Do the Next Thing

For Elisabeth Shirey, my daughter and
Elisabeth Elliot's namesake, and for my
grandchildren, Winston, Cedric, Zoe, and
Ransom, and hopefully many more to come.

Do the Next Thing

Elisabeth Elliot

Selah Helms

CF4·K

10 9 8 7 6 5 4 3 2 1

Copyright 2018 Selah Helms

Paperback ISBN: 978-1-5271-0161-6

epub ISBN: 978-1-5271-0216-3

mobi ISBN: 978-1-5271-0217-0

Published by

Christian Focus Publications,

Geanies House, Fearn, Tain, Ross-shire,

IV20 1TW, Scotland, U.K.

www.christianfocus.com

email: info@christianfocus.com

Printed and bound by Nørhaven, Denmark

Cover design by Daniel van Straaten

Contents

Acknowledgements

The author is indebted to Elisabeth's husband Lars for many interviews, conversations, and guidance during the research process. Also, the Billy Graham Center archives at Wheaton College provided invaluable help as a resource on her thoughts and life. Scripture quotations are in the Amplified Version, NIV, Phillips and King James Version of the Bible. Footnoted quotes in dialogue are literal, direct quotes from Elisabeth's speeches, writings, and correspondence. Other dialogue is drawn from thoughts that appear frequently in her writings and speaking.

Missionary from the Start

The young mother clapped a lid on a box and scanned the small apartment hurriedly.

"I think this is the last of it," she told herself. "What have I forgotten?" The three rooms stared back at her, the massive antique furniture holding a wealth of memories.

She and her missionary husband had been happy in the five years they had lived in Brussels—first for a few years in an old, run-down building, fifty-eight steps above a wine shop, and with no running water; next, for a few months in a three room apartment heated by coal, the bathtub in the kitchen. They had learned French and explained the gospel to children in the slums of Brussels. They had taught Bible classes. After they had been there for over a year, Katherine had learned she was to have a baby; young Phil joined them on the mission field. He was now packed up for travel and was with his father, also named Phil, waiting for her at the dock.

Phil's care had taken up much of her time, and, as a result, she felt she was a poor specimen of a missionary. She had been asked to teach a group of women but was not sure she had been up to it. She wrote her parents back home, "I tried to wriggle out of it but Philippians 4:13 kept recurring to me, *'I can do all things through Christ which strengtheneth me'*(KJV), until I finally had to say I'd try to do it. I've since wondered what the ladies got out of my feeble efforts, but I know the experience was good for me."[1]

Then baby Elisabeth had come along as well.

Now Katherine remembered she must rush to meet her husband. She snatched up the box and headed for the door. The motorcar hummed impatiently as she jumped inside.

"What have I forgotten? Anything?" she called back to the maid. "I'm headed to the docks."

"Wait, madam, you have forgotten something!" The maid ran to the car with a bundle in her arms. "The baby, madam! Think about the baby!"

Katherine nodded. "Yes, yes, of course." She met the maid and gathered her tiny daughter into her arms. Elisabeth was five months old. Her mother bundled her snugly for protection from the brisk Belgian wind and in minutes joined her husband at the docks. There, they would ferry to England and then take a steamer home. The voyage would take about a week to reach the shores of the United States.

---

1. Elisabeth Elliot, *The Shaping of a Christian Family* (Nashville: Thomas Nelson, 1992), p. 48.

As they boarded the ship, an event was unfolding three thousand miles away that would change their world forever. A young man took off in a specially designed aircraft from the coast of Long Island, New York. The plane was heavy with fuel and barely made it over the telephone wires at the end of the runway. Five hundred people watched as young Charles Lindbergh headed out toward the Atlantic Ocean, his silver "Spirit of St. Louis" gleaming in the morning sky. No one had ever crossed the Atlantic in an airplane before. Others had tried and died in the attempt. It was his try now. He had slimmed his equipment down to carry as little extra weight as possible. He packed four sandwiches, one canteen, and put a wicker chair in the cockpit.

The trip would take thirty-six hours. Charles fought sleep all along the way. He encountered dense fog and attempted to fly above it, then under it. During the times he tried to figure out where he was, he would drop down to twenty feet above the leaping waves to get his bearings. Once, his plane started icing up, and he was sure he would be lost at sea.

"That worried me a great deal," Lindbergh later wrote, "and I debated whether I should keep on or go back. I decided I must not think any more about going back."[2]

On the second day, he thought he was close to the coast of England when he saw fishing boats and

2. *"The Flight"* Charles Lindbergh An American Aviator, http://www.charleslindbergh.com/history/paris.asp.

swooped down close to ask directions. But he couldn't make out what they said in response.

Finally he spotted the coastline of France. From there, he followed the Seine River to Paris. The Eiffel Tower loomed into view; he saw a cheering crowd waiting. As he spiraled down, descending to land, one hundred thousand people broke through police barricades and swarmed the runway. There were so many right beneath his plane, he was afraid the propeller might hit them.

Speeches, awards, and honor awaited Charles Lindbergh. He had opened up a new era of travel. Suddenly, the world would feel like a much smaller place because airplanes could get people wherever they wanted to go, and quickly. They could shorten the distances from country to country, continent to continent, and reach out-of-the-way places that were inaccessible by car, boat, or foot. The breakthrough would prove a vital help to the cause of missions. With the ability to travel by airplane, missionaries could reach people groups who had never heard the gospel or even had any contact with the modern world. Jets, rocket ships, and space shuttles were yet to be developed, but the little aircraft Lindbergh flew in 1927 was much like the ones missionaries would use for decades.

Katherine and Phil and their little ones disembarked onto American shores to the news of Lindbergh's success. Could they have known then how his flight would affect their lives? Could this missionary couple have suspected that their little Elisabeth would one day join a team of hardy young pioneer missionaries who would take the gospel to peoples so primitive that no white man had ever associated with them and lived to tell about it? Could they have known that their baby daughter would one day use the same sort of plane to reach a fierce, remote people, forging a story that would be heard around the world, and raising up a new generation of missionaries that were eager to lay down their lives for the kingdom of God?

An Eye for Detail

"Come, Betts, listen with me." Her father called Elisabeth by her pet name, taking her hand and gently drawing her to sit on a cool, grey rock in the woods where they walked.

"Shush," he said, "do you hear that bird calling?"

"Yes, Daddy, I think it's a wood thrush," Elisabeth replied. "It sounds like a beautiful bell."

"Very good," her father gazed down on her proudly. "The wood thrush is chubby and polka-dotted over his belly," he said. "You can see him perched in that Chinese chestnut tree over there."

"Where?" she looked through the array of green colors down the hill.

"There, the chestnut tree has leaves like fingers."

She nodded in excitement. "Yes, there he is."

Then her father lowered his voice and sang out a bird call of his own.

"It's the crested flycatcher!" she said excitedly.

"Right again!" he said. Across the trees, they heard melodic tones resembling a piccolo.

"That's the song sparrow, little Betts," said her father. He mimicked the call perfectly. "See, you hold your mouth like this."

Elisabeth laughed. It was so much fun to go on a walk with her father. He knew all the birds and trees and loved to teach them to his children.

In the time since they had moved back to the States, their father had become a writer and editor for the *Sunday School Times*, an aid that went out from Philadelphia to Sunday School teachers in churches of all kinds throughout the country. His eye for detail made for descriptive and colorful writing, and he was well-respected in the ministry.

When Elisabeth's father would return home from work every day, Katherine, her mother, would gather the children for supper and family devotions. By now, the Howard family had grown. It was 1934. Phil was now ten, Elisabeth was seven, and Dave was six.

At the supper table that night, her father opened as he always did. "Our Father, we thank Thee for this good food, and with this we ask Thy blessing, in the name of our Lord Jesus Christ, amen."

Parents and children engaged in lively but orderly conversation around the dining table, not interrupting each other, but taking turns. Frequent laughter peppered their amiable chit chat.

Mr Howard asked his daughter how school was going.

"It's fine, Daddy. Sometimes arithmetic is hard for me to figure out." Elisabeth squirmed a little in her seat.

She didn't really enjoy math. She liked words like her daddy did. Suddenly she had an idea that would divert the focus away from math.

"Like Miss Maclean says, "Oyful! It's poifectly oyful when a poyson can't do theah homewoyk." Elisabeth's nasal tones perfectly reflected her Sunday School teacher's thick New Jersey accent, showing the skill of mimicry she had picked up from her father (with birds) and then put her own spin on (with people).

"Now, Betty, she's a devoted soul,"[1] her mother cautioned, gently curbing the fun Elisabeth was making at someone else's expense.

"Let's get to family prayers now, children." Her father directed his oldest son to the hymnals, while he pulled the little volume of *Daily Light* off the buffet table. Mr Howard turned to the evening portion for that date and read the short selection of Scripture. The three children listened quietly and attentively. When he had concluded, Mr Howard asked a few questions to see how well his children had been listening and how well they understood.

"Now, everyone, what are your prayer requests?" he asked.

"Could you pray I could finish my schoolwork in time to get to play baseball in the evenings?" Phil asked. Mr Howard wrote it down.

"How about you, Dearie?"

---

1. *Elisabeth Elliot Memorial Service at Wheaton College*, https://www.youtube.com/watch?v=WSi3mR9GQIE

Their mother spoke mildly. "Please pray for my strength in caring for the children."

Elisabeth thought hard. She remembered what she thought was a baby hospital down the street from their house. Sometimes she heard crying coming through the windows.

"I'd like to ask prayer for a baby sister," she piped up. "We could get one from that baby home down the street."

Her parents looked at each other. "Well, that's not how we got the rest of you," her mother explained. "God can make a baby grow inside the mother."[2]

"Then, that's what I want to ask for," said Elisabeth. "I want the Lord to grow me a sister."

Their eyes all closed in prayer and her father's rich tones met her ears. "Bless dear Mother, give her strength for her work; bless Phil in his schoolwork, help Betty with hers—especially her arithmetic.[3] Help Davey be an obedient boy. In the name of our Lord Jesus Christ, who taught us to pray." Then the family joined him, heads bowed still, in reciting the Lord's prayer.

Now came the singing. Young Phil asked for "Savior, Like a Shepherd Lead Us." Together, the family sang through every verse. The next night, another child would get a turn to choose a hymn for the family to sing, again, through all the verses. By this practice, the children quickly learned many hymns by memory.

2. Elisabeth Elliot, *The Shaping of a Christian Family* (Nashville: Thomas Nelson, 1992), p. 81.
3. Ibid., p. 59.

And the task was completely painless. They loved to sing together.

A few weeks later, Elisabeth woke up to the smell of bacon frying. Aunt Alice, the family's household helper, called upstairs for the children to come down for breakfast. The winter chill in Elisabeth's bedroom made her reluctant to leave her bed.

"Come down, Phil, Betty, Davey! Come and eat. Your mother and daddy are away for the morning."

The children came downstairs shivering. They tried to busy themselves as they waited for their parents to return. Davey, the most mischievous of the three, began fiddling with a stick. The stick had been wedged in tightly to keep the window panes shut in their proper position, and he wanted the window open. As he forced it open, the upper frame descended with a crash. Glass shattered everywhere. Elisabeth and Phil groaned as the biting winter wind roared into the room. Aunt Alice had to call for a repairman, but it would be several hours before he could come. The children picked up the braided rug and huddled under it, cold and miserable for the rest of the day, wishing their parents would come back.

After a while, the telephone rang, and Aunt Alice went to answer it.

"It's for you, children!" she called out. They ran to the phone in the hallway.

"Phil, Betts, Dave," said their dad breathlessly, "Your mother is fine. We have a new baby in the family. Betts,

God has answered your prayer. He has given you a baby sister. Her name is Virginia Anne. We'll call her Ginny."

"Thank you, Lord," Elisabeth prayed that night. The Lord is real, she thought. He can be trusted. He is with my family and He cares for me too. He notices even the details of my life, just like my father. Thus, Elisabeth's early impressions of the Lord were formed by a peaceful home and loving parents.

Disobedience During Singing

Over the next few years, there were several more changes in store for the Howard family. A year after baby Ginny's birth, baby Thomas arrived. The Howards bought their first car. And to the great delight of the children, their parents moved the family to a new, bigger house.

Their old backyard was as small as a "pocket-sized handkerchief" said their mother, which had proved a challenge in keeping them contained. "The boys had sled wagons and scooted up and down the street and sometimes coasted down the hilly part of McCallum Street, endangering not only their own lives but those of innocent old ladies and small tots as well."[1]

The children needed more room to run and play. In the large old New Jersey house they moved to, there were seventeen rooms. Phil picked the upstairs screened-in porch for his bedroom. There was a glass-enclosed room where the dog slept and where blocks could be built into cities. There was a place for a piano,

1. Ibid, p. 83.

where the children could learn to accompany the family hymn-sings. Two garages made room for their tricycles and bikes and sleds and wagons. There were dogwood and poplar and beech trees waiting to be climbed and a dirt patch perfect for building bridges and houses and running cars. They named their new house "Birdsong."

Yet the children were expected to come instantly when called, no matter how much fun they were having. Excuses or delay were viewed as disobedience.

"Tommy, come pick up the blocks you left out before supper time," his mom called out one day.

"But Mommy, I'm busy. I'm playing 'Jesus Loves me' on the piano," he sweetly replied.

His father's frame filled the doorway. "Now Tommy, it's no use singing songs for the Lord if you are being disobedient," he said. "It's no good preaching if you haven't swept your floor."

Tommy complied. Though the home was aglow with active play, it was orderly and clean.

Davey was still the most rascally member of the family. Sometimes that boy could be downright flippant. One week, he kept coming just to the edge of disobedience with little needling things to annoy and irritate his siblings, not all of which merited a spanking. By Wednesday, his mom approached him.

"Son, you seem to be tuning up for a spanking!"[2]

Davey smiled. Maybe he would calm down for a bit. But the temptation to annoy proved irresistible.

---

2. Elisabeth Elliot, *"Serenity,"* CD Lars Gren Collection.

"Davey," his mom was stern. "I have my stick handy, and I'm going to use it!"[3]

"Well, I have my legs handy, and I'm going to use them,"[4] came his retort. His mom was amused, but she doled out the prescribed consequences nonetheless. Perhaps she gave him an extra swat for the sass on top of the disobedience?

Another time, Katherine had to tell her young son, "Davey, sit on that chair in your bedroom until I tell you to get up." She knew he needed some time out to reflect on his behavior, and to give his siblings a break. She stressed that he must not leave the chair. Minutes later, she returned to his room to check on him. Davey wasn't there, and the chair wasn't there either.

Downstairs, the phone rang. It was the neighbor across the street. "Katherine," she exclaimed. "Did you know that one of your sons is sitting in a chair on the roof of your house?"[5] Katherine gasped and ran outside to see Davey far above her reach.

"I didn't leave the chair, Mother!" Davey shouted down triumphantly.

Yes, Davey was a handful.

Elisabeth was different though. She was shy and tall for her age and felt like she was in the way. Sometimes, especially when they had company, she would rather stay in the shadows and watch. When asked to help with

---

3. Ibid.
4. Ibid.
5. Ibid.

a chore, her temptation was to give her mother reasons why she was unable to comply. There were simply other things she'd rather do with her time.

"Don't debate me or give me six reasons why you can't do it," Katherine would say. "Just do what I say."[6]

It was a challenge for Elisabeth to keep a yielded spirit. But she really wanted to do it.

Elisabeth was twelve when she copied down this prayer in her Bible: "Lord, I give up all my own plans, purposes, desires for my life and accept your will for my life. Use me as Thou wilt. Send me where Thou wilt at any cost whatever."[7]

She had first heard this prayer when still very small, the day Betty Scott had come for supper. Missionaries were frequent dinner guests in the Howard home, and the Howard children loved to hear their stories. Betty Scott's story had left a deep imprint on Elisabeth. Betty and her future husband John Stam would be traveling to China to bring the gospel to rural Chinese people. But the year they went to China, there was great unrest all over the country. A revolution had left the people vulnerable to rampaging soldiers.

"I have asked the Lord to use my life however He will," Betty Scott told the young Howards. "My life means nothing to me. My only desire is that my whole life be given to the service of my Master."

---

6. Ibid.
7. Elisabeth Elliot, *"Stronghold of My Life,"* CD Lars Gren Collection.

Elisabeth Elliot*Elisabeth Elliot*

John and Betty had then married and left the safe shores of America, knowing they would be entering dangerous ground—a war zone. Elisabeth had been about seven when, months later, she heard the report that shortly after arriving in China, the young missionary couple had been marched partially clad through the streets by rough, communist soldiers and had been beheaded as they knelt together on a hill outside the town. Their three-month-old baby had been rescued and kept hidden by nationals until she could be smuggled home to her grieving grandparents. Elisabeth recognized early that giving your life to the Lord meant serious business.

25

Good Missionary Training

Missionaries were heroes to the Howard children, and they used their chores and self-imposed projects to toughen themselves up to be like those brave men and women. "GMT," they called it. "Good Missionary Training."

As Elisabeth matured, she kept her ears open for older, wiser believers who might teach her more about yielding her unruly spirit to the Lord. She was a teenager now, and her youngest brother had just been born. Elisabeth knew now, that as her mother was getting older, having a new baby would be a little harder on her. When not busy with her school work, she made sure to help her mother around the house, even though she didn't always want to do it.

One day, she kept an eye on Jim in his little rocking duck. The long veranda on which it sat went all alongside the house, and there was plenty of room for Elisabeth to curl up with a book while she helped her mother with the baby. The little rocking duck was furiously creaking, scooting along the wooden floor boards with the baby's zealous exertions. Elisabeth could see the sunlight make dancing shadows at the base of the toy. After a while, the creaking slowed. Then Jim revived with another burst of energy, though for a briefer time. Then another, even less enthusiastic, burst of speed. Finally, the creaking stopped as little Jim fell asleep. Her mother emerged from the kitchen, her hands dusty with flour.

They both laughed at the baby, now leaning limply over the side of the rocking duck, fast asleep.

"Mother, I have a question," said Elisabeth. These times out on the porch were perfect for musing.

"Yes, dearie, what is it?" her mother responded. Katherine could always be depended on for a cheerful response. Sometimes, it seemed to Elisabeth that all of her mother's sentences ended in exclamation marks.

"Well, we've had so many missionaries come into our home," she began. "And they tell us all about their marvelous adventures. But mother," she frowned, "they are all such regular people. They're not snobbish. They don't sugarcoat their work.

"Mr Abel told us about how the tribes he worked with actually ate each other! But he also swung us around in a chair—he was a joy to be with. Mr and Mrs Sutherland told us about the people from China who were coming to know the Lord. And they taught us how to climb a mountain in China just like the Chinese do, putting a little bounce into each step."

She went on. "And Miss Stepanian told us about how her whole family was killed in the Turkish massacre, and how she alone was saved by Bedouins, and lived with them in tents in the desert. But my, how she could fill our living room with her rich soprano voice during our hymn-sings.

"But, I don't understand," Elisabeth continued. "When you hear about missionaries in churches and at meetings, they're made to sound so 'other worldly.'

"Missionaries don't 'work,' they 'labor.'" Elisabeth was always picking up on other people's words. "And they don't just 'go,' they 'go forth!'" She was standing up on the porch and making flowing gestures with her hands now. "And they don't 'walk,' they 'tread the burning sands.' Mother, it all sounds so unnatural and pretentious!"

Her mother's response calmed her once again. "Now, Betts, I know it sounds that way. Sometimes God's people do tend to think of missions rather romantically. But somehow, despite the sentimentality, the Lord's work still gets done."[1]

Elisabeth knew her mother was right. Still, she liked things to be straightforward and unvarnished. Sure, she wanted to serve the Lord, but let service to Him be spoken of honestly!

Her uncle, a widely traveled public speaker, came for a visit to see the new baby. While at their house, he

---

1. Elisabeth Elliot, *"My Life for Others,"* Urbana 1996,
https://www.youtube.com/watch?v=0Q4X_DOT0d0

described a boarding school he'd visited in Florida. The students there were trained in the Bible and in good manners. They learned ballroom dancing and rode horses. They were given opportunities to serve others. They learned strong Christian behavior and values. They learned about missionaries. This Hampden DuBose Boarding School really captured Elisabeth's imagination. Surely her fledgling Christian yearnings would grow in a place like that. At fourteen years old, she asked her parents if she might go there and attend school. Since her uncle had recommended it so highly, they were willing. Though she would miss Birdsong, she was eager for this next chance to learn in her life.

Elisabeth little knew then how stern these new lessons would prove to be!

* * *

"Betty Howard! You are so negative," the headmistress, Mrs DuBose, told her. "You can do anything in the world that you want to do. The problem is, you don't want to!"[2] The same old lesson, thought Elisabeth, but even more bracing when someone other than her mother said it.

"Betty Howard! You are self-conscious," the older woman scolded her one day. "And the only reason you are self-conscious is because you are selfish. It's pure selfishness!"[3]

---

2. Elisabeth Elliot, *"Stronghold of My Life,"* CD Lars Gren Collection.

3. Elisabeth Elliot, *"Loving Providence,"* CD Lars Gren Collection.

"No, that can't be why I'm quiet!" Elisabeth balked. "I just prefer not to make a scene." Elisabeth was much taller now as a teenager than she was as a child. She towered over many of the boys her age. How could she not feel self-conscious about that?

"You can get over your self-consciousness or we will help you pack your bags and give you a ride to the train station," the older woman was relentless. "We don't need you at this school!"[4]

Ouch. These were painful lessons. But Elisabeth did so want to grow and learn to be more useful in the hands of the Lord. And hadn't she said she liked straightforward talk? She went forward at the end of every chapel service, joining the other young people at the altar, offering her life up to the Lord. She knew the Lord wanted her to get past her shy awkwardness and learn to be bold with His Word. She hoped He would indeed use her on the mission field.

As the Lord would have it, Mrs DuBose ended up being a source of great encouragement to Elisabeth. During the school's vespers services, the older woman aimed to give her young charges a taste of missionary words. She often quoted from the writings of a missionary to India named Amy Carmichael. Elisabeth was enthralled. Here was a woman without fluff and flightiness talking straight to her about the rigors of discipleship.

4. Ibid.

"Mrs DuBose, Miss Carmichael's words speak to me," Elisabeth approached her headmistress timidly one day. "They're captivating!"

"Yes, child, I am glad you like her! Here, I'll loan you some of her books."

Amy Carmichael's writing rang with unvarnished clarity, as well as beauty, to Elisabeth's word-trained ears. She spoke of the rigors like a real person, just like the Howards' missionary friends, with genuineness and with a pure heart toward God. There was nothing of man-centered mush in Amy Carmichael! Elisabeth devoured the books.

> If I covet any place on earth but the
> dust at the foot of the cross,
> then I know nothing of Calvary love.
> "If the ultimate, the hardest, cannot be asked of me;
> if my fellows hesitate to ask it and turn to someone else,
> then I know nothing of Calvary love.

Elisabeth began to memorize the poems of this womanly hero. Amy became like a spiritual mother to her. One poem especially stood out to Elisabeth because it spoke directly to her battle with yielding her strong will to the Lord.

In Acceptance Lieth Peace

> He said, 'I will forget the dying faces;
> The empty places,
> They shall be filled again.
> O voices moaning deep within me, cease.'

But vain the word; vain, vain:
Not in forgetting lieth peace.

He said, 'I will crowd action upon action,
The strife of faction
Shall stir me and sustain;
O tears that drown the fire of manhood cease.'
But vain the word; vain, vain:
Not in endeavour lieth peace.

He said, 'I will withdraw me and be quiet,
Why meddle in life's riot?
Shut be my door to pain.
Desire, thou dost befool me, thou shalt cease.'
But vain the word; vain, vain:
Not in aloofness lieth peace.

He said, 'I will submit; I am defeated.
God hath depleted
My life of its rich gain.
O futile murmurings, why will ye not cease?'
But vain the word; vain, vain:
Not in submission lieth peace.

He said, 'I will accept the breaking sorrow
Which God tomorrow
Will to His son explain.'
Then did the turmoil deep within me cease.
Not vain the word, not vain;
For in Acceptance lieth peace."

Amy Carmichael

Yes, this was it! She needed to learn total acceptance of things God wanted her to do and become. Oh, how she desired this same spirit! She realized from Amy's words that a person could be very strong and yet yielded at the same time.

"There's so much [out there] that's wishy-washy … but there is something pure and steel-like in Amy Carmichael, [in her] absolutely flint-like determination to be obedient,"[5] Elisabeth said later.

She was hooked and humbled. How gracious the Lord was to keep working with her!

Yes, her time at Hampden proved to be good missionary training all the way around.

---

5. Interview with Elisabeth Howard Gren, March 26, 1985. Tape T2, Collection 278, Papers of Elisabeth Howard Gren, Archives of the Billy Graham Center, Wheaton, Illinois.

A Pure Passion

Elisabeth sat focused, pen on paper, before her open textbook in the student center. She was at Wheaton College now. The Lord had confirmed to her during her time here that she was indeed called to be a missionary. She had yielded her life to bring the gospel to tribes without a copy of the Bible in their own language. She had prayed the prayer of Chinese missionary Betty Scott when she was a little girl. During her time at Hampden, she had absorbed the no-nonsense walk with God from Amy Carmichael. (Little did she know that in years to come, after she had left Hampden, Mrs Dubose would hold out Elisabeth Howard's example as a model for new students to follow.) Now she was at Wheaton to become fluent in classical Greek—a good background for translating the New Testament into the languages of various people groups. Perhaps in Africa? Or South America? She didn't know where just yet. So she focused on the Greek sentence in front of her.

"*Hippocrates had got half through the army with his …*"[1] What? She was pretty sure that the next word translated into something like "exhortation." She was translating her way skillfully through Thucydides' Greek history book. The influence of her dad's love for words was definitely making her Greek studies easier. Words came to her like second nature. So, on to the next phrase: "*when the Boeotians, after a few more hasty words from Pagaondas, …*" (those were proper names, she was sure) "*… struck up the paean.*"[2]

Now what was "paean" again? At that moment, another copy of Thucydides, just like hers, hit the table with a friendly smack. She looked up into the eyes of Jim Elliot.

"What are we covering today?" he asked jauntily.

"What do you mean, what are we covering? I'm still in the eighth year of the Peloponnesian War." Elisabeth hovered between two feelings. She couldn't decide whether to be annoyed or attracted. "I think you are about six pages behind," she said wryly.

"I'd like to join you," he said.

Elisabeth motioned to the chair beside her. "Go ahead." Jim was admired by all the college girls. He was strikingly handsome. He was a wrestler; his neck was thick and his muscles large. But though he was generally well-liked, he had the reputation of being a

---

1. Robert Strassler, editor, *The Landmark Thucydides, A Newly Revised Edition of the Richard Crawley Translation* (New York: Simon and Shuster, 1996), p. 275.
2. Ibid.

"woman-hater." He had somehow got it in his mind that to devote his life wholeheartedly to the Lord, he had to say no to dating and marriage. So, many girls' hopes were disappointed.

Jim was in several of Elisabeth's classes this semester. He was a Greek major too and headed for missions. As he sat down beside her, she suspected that he just wanted her to do most of the work, since he struggled with the language more than she did. After all, she considered herself a wallflower at school, still tall and awkward and way too quiet to be one of the "in" crowd—certainly not a girl that a man like Jim Elliot would notice! She just didn't know what to make of his friendly overtures toward her.

"Well, do you remember what the word 'paean' means?" she asked him, business-like and proper. Together they bent over the ancient text.

"I think it's a kind of chant to rally the soldiers," Jim said. "Let's look it up." With dictionary in hand, they worked through a few sentences. Elisabeth was attentive to his zeal for the Lord—it piqued her interest. But she was not sure why he wanted to study with her. Over the weeks, it seemed to her that he showed up wherever she was, but she wasn't sure.

Jim was not sure what he thought of Elisabeth either. He wrote home to his parents, "Betty is the sledgehammer type of personality when she knows you, though she may appear quiet at first glance. She is blunt and dominating and this makes her tend to domineer, but I can't explain her."[3]

Jim had befriended Dave, Elisabeth's now-grown brother. And when Dave invited Jim home for the Christmas holiday, Jim was very impressed with the Howard family. They were godly and serious about life. Somehow he and Elisabeth formed a "thought-bond," as Jim described it, that he had known with few others. They agreed on almost everything, it seemed, little things and life-changing things. He was confused, because he had decided to go to the mission field unmarried. She had too. Yet, somehow, she found herself growing more attached to this Jim Elliot.

"I have just come in from a long talk with Betty Howard," he wrote his parents. "Somehow she is deliciously satisfying company—and this, strangely enough, is not on account of a fine-featured face, a shapely form, not even on account of rare conversational powers. Of the former two she possesses very little appeal."[4]

Elisabeth was trying to keep her expectations in check. She admired Jim tremendously because of his rugged devotion to obeying God and his manly zeal for tackling missions. Jim asked Elisabeth out on one date during the spring semester. Of course, it was a date to church to listen to a missionary! That

---

3. Elisabeth Elliot, *Shadow of the Almighty* (San Francisco: Harper & Row, 1958), p. 75.
4. Ibid., p. 67

night, C.T. Studd's daughter told of his death in a remote hut in Africa. That's what discipleship meant to Elisabeth: going to live, and possibly die, in a hut in some distant place—surrendering to the will of God everything she had or wanted. So Elisabeth tried to keep her focus on Greek in spite of a faintly disturbing concern that she might be falling in love with one Jim Elliot.

Her heart beat wildly late one evening when he asked to meet her for a coke down at the student center. Yes, she said, she'd love to. She jumped at the chance.

But when he sat down beside her, there was no beginning flicker of a romantic flame. Instead, he gave her a friendly rebuke.

"Betts," he spoke, "You are my sister in Christ." He spoke forthrightly (as she had previously prided herself on appreciating), "I think you are too inward. You need to be more friendly to people. You need to love people more."

She sighed, and reluctantly thanked him. Perhaps straightforward talk did have its drawbacks, especially when a girl was hoping for something else. But she did take his mild scolding to heart, and soon she joined the crowd from campus that went on witnessing trips to neighboring areas. That would be a good way to improve on her boldness. She hoped Jim wouldn't think she accompanied the group out of a desire just to be near him. First and foremost, she wanted to grow because the Lord wanted her to grow.

Another day, she shyly asked Jim to write in her class year book.

"*2 Timothy 2:4, Jim,*" he jotted down beside his photograph. It was so brief! Elisabeth hurried back to her dorm room to look up the Scripture he mentioned. She quickly found the place in her Bible: "*No soldier in active service gets entangled in the [ordinary business] affairs of civilian life; [he avoids them] so that he may please the one who enlisted him to serve.*" (AMP)

"Oh my," she thought, "that doesn't sound like he's thinking about marriage at all." She had hoped that the reference would contain a sort of hidden message to her that would hint of things to come in their friendship, things more than mere friendship. That night, Elisabeth repeated her familiar prayer. "Lord, my life is yours completely. Do whatever you will with me. I will accept it if you do not have Jim Elliot in my future." A yielded heart, that's what she wanted, even more than she wanted Jim. "*In acceptance lieth peace.*"

A Passion Denied

It soon came time for Elisabeth to graduate from Wheaton College. It was 1948. For over a year, she'd been trying to rein in her galloping emotions concerning Jim. She filled her journals with Scripture to keep her thoughts on the Lord. She prayed and cried. Her quietness served her well, because no one but the Lord needed to know how much she really wanted Jim, least of all, Jim himself. He was still set on a single life on some foreign mission field. And the Lord would help her to keep her friendship and future with Jim Elliot in its proper place—under the feet of her Lord Jesus.

The missions club at the school hosted a last Memorial Day picnic before the summer holiday. Elisabeth stayed behind afterward to help clean up. As she took a last load of hotdog wrappers and coke bottles to the trash bin, she caught Jim looking at her curiously from a perch atop a picnic table. His legs swung back and forth in his focused, energetic way.

"Walk you home?" Jim rose and came over to her.

"Sure," she said. But he was unusually quiet on the walk back to school. And she didn't know what to say. She watched him from the corner of her eye as they continued along their silent way.

At last, he began. "Betts ... we've got to get squared away on how we feel about each other." [1]

Elisabeth was shocked. So he had feelings for her?! She never would have guessed, never dared hope. But here he was, acting as if things were understood on both their parts.

"Feel about each other?! You mean—?" [2]

"Now come on Bett. Don't tell me you didn't know that I was in love with you?" [3] he contended.

"I had no idea," [4] she insisted.

"Really? But you must have! I've been knocking myself out to be with you, be nice to you, show you how I felt without actually saying anything. You mean you didn't notice?" [5]

"I noticed," she said slowly. "But I was afraid to believe my eyes. I told myself you couldn't possibly be interested, let alone—" [6]

"In love. That's what I'm telling you." [7]

They talked for hours over the next several days.

---

1. Elisabeth Elliot, *Passion and Purity* (Grand Rapids: Fleming H. Revell, 1984),p. 52.
2. Ibid.
3. Ibid.
4. Ibid.
5. Ibid.
6. Ibid.
7. Ibid.

Somehow, Elisabeth tried to wrap her mind around all that Jim was saying to her. He loved her. He wanted her. He told her so. It was the glorious state of affairs she had refused to allow herself to dream about. Yet, somehow, he was still committed to a single life. Single missionaries were available to do things married ones could not, he explained to her. He would not get married unless God somehow clearly revealed to him that he should.

"If I marry, I know who it'll be. That is, of course, if she'll have me."[8] Jim's smile melted her heart. She smiled in return but said nothing.

"But I'm not asking," he hurried on. "I can't do that, Bett, and you'll have to understand that. I can't ask you to marry me. I can't even ask you to wait. I've given you and all my feelings for you to God. He'll have to work out whatever He wants."[9]

"Impossible man!" Elisabeth thought to herself. How exactly would the Lord show him anything? She didn't know whether to jump for joy or to wilt in tears. Yet, here it was again, the chance to wait silently on the Lord, the chance to trust Him with her life. Even though she had what she thought she wanted so dearly—Jim's love—nothing ever took away the need to trust that the Lord knew best for her life. For "in acceptance lieth peace." She retrieved her copy of Amy Carmichael's poetry. The plain words of the old saint steadied her shaky soul.

8. Ibid., p. 56
9. Ibid.

A few nights later, Jim and Elisabeth again took a walk and shared their love for each other. Their talks led them wandering into a cemetery. Together they sat down on a stone slab. The worn rectangular headstones reminded Elisabeth of the helplessness of life. None of us has control over his life, she thought. All must be submitted to Jesus.

"Jim," she said, "I don't think we should continue to communicate with each other for a while, or at least not very often." She wanted so badly to reach for his hand, but held back. "I think that talking with each other will just make this harder, as long as the future is unclear."

Jim fell silent for a long time. "I agree," he said faintly. "This morning I read about Abraham's sacrifice of Isaac to the Lord. He was his father's dearest treasure. Yet Abraham gave him up willingly. I give you to the Lord, dear Betts. You are not mine, and I will not treat you as if you were. You belong to our Lord."

They lingered in the moonlight for what seemed like hours. As the moon slowly rose over the two solemn young people, the shadows lengthened off the silent gray stones. Both of them watched in hushed wonder while the long silhouette of a nearby cross fell between their own dark figures across the stone on which they sat. They marveled together. Was it a sign from the Lord? In future years, Elisabeth could never speak of it without weeping.

When the Lord Builds the House

Elisabeth sat on the large wooden platform that somehow passed as her bed. Though the frame was large enough for a double-sized mattress, only a twin mattress, stuffed with hard-packed cotton, provided the place where she sat. On the remainder of the platform, where a larger mattress would have lain, she stored her Bible, her pen, and a little camping lantern that served as her bedside lamp. She was finally on the mission field. And surely the Lord had brought her here as a missionary to Ecuador and had planned great works here for her and the three young ladies who served with her. Her friends would teach the Colorado Indian children to read and write, would treat their diseases—many brought in by white explorers—and would teach them the stories of the Bible. Her job would be to work on transcribing the sounds of the Indian language into words on paper, toward the ultimate goal of translating the New Testament into their musical language, so they could have a copy of the Scriptures they could read for themselves.

She shook the strange bugs out of the paper on her lap and continued her letter—to Jim. When they had parted ways at Wheaton, she had gone on to gain some further language training in Oklahoma, then she had traveled to Brooklyn, New York, to hone her Spanish skills by living in a Spanish-speaking community there. For these few years, she had lived in constant loneliness. She would try to pray, and end up thinking of Jim. She would try to concentrate on her studies, only to think of Jim. She would intend to serve the Lord wholeheartedly, but when she was around others who were married, she thought of Jim.

Then she had finally set sail for Ecuador. There she lived in Quito—one of the busier, modern places in the country—for several months, still working on her Spanish. Jim was there, doing the same. Together, they raced through their language studies, pitted against each other in a friendly competition to see who could get to the mission field first. After class each day, they had time to walk and see the sights. Her love for him had grown. And now, as excited as she was to be in San Miguel de los Colorados, putting her language skills into action, she thought surely it would be a temporary thing. Surely the Lord would lead Jim to marry her soon. Then they could serve as missionaries together.

She described her room to him in her letter. Though presumably the bamboo walls reached to the ceiling, she suspected that way up at the top, the boards didn't meet. When she tried to sleep at nights, she could hear swishing sounds of wings above her head as fruit bats and various insects found their way inside her room. That gap between the ceiling and the walls—she lamented that at night.

But perhaps she and Jim would build a home of their own soon. They had been drawn together like magnets during their time in Quito.

In the meantime, she had the language to learn.

"Why do you paint your bodies black?" she would ask the Indians, to engage them in conversation. She must learn the language.

"Why do you not paint your body black?" they would ask in return. Not much progress there.

"Why do you paint your teeth and tongue black?" she tried again. They gave a similar answer. Eventually, she pieced together that it had something to do with being less noticeable to animals they hunted. She wondered if their bright red hair or their yellow and turquoise scarves might prove a forewarning to the animals, despite their otherwise shrewd intentions.

Sometimes she asked about the birds. The Indians could always seem to find them in the trees when her eyes failed her. How could she miss them when so many of them were so colorful—orange and black and bright green? If only she could show these birds to her father. He would love learning to imitate their calls. She listened to the croaking noises of the toucan and the soft conversation of the parrots. Their communal chatter, high in the trees, reminded her of the sounds of happy children playing. If only she could pick up so easily on the sounds of the Colorado language. She tried to make the most of the few chats she had with the Colorados who came through the mission station. It was not easy.

One day, she met a young Ecuadorian man named Don Macario. Don Macario was specially sent by the Lord, Elisabeth just knew. He came from a Spanish-speaking family, but he had played with Colorado children growing up. This made him fluent in exactly the two languages Elisabeth needed him to be fluent in. Better still, he was a Christian, so he was actually excited about helping her translate the Bible for his fellow countrymen. And he had been looking for a way to serve the Lord. This seemed the perfect opportunity to him. Elisabeth was delighted when he agreed to help her put the language on paper.

Together, they set up a table and two chairs in a small schoolroom. Elisabeth got her index cards, a little wooden recipe box, and pencil, then sat down to work.

It was slow going. When she asked the Indian to give her words for nouns, things went pretty well. She could point to the dish of roasted plaintain, cooked in ashes, that the Indians often ate, and easily learn the word for it.

"Que es eso?" she would ask. "What is that?"

"Ano," he would answer. "The word for plaintain is 'ano.'"

"Que es eso?" she would ask again, pointing out the window to a skinny dog foraging through the kitchen trash.

"Susu," he would answer. So the word for dog was 'susu.' She quickly wrote it down.

She pointed to one of the schoolchildren running outside, newly freed by the clanging school bell.

"Na," he said. So that's the word for 'child.' She wrote another card, with the English word alongside. Her little wooden box swelled with new cards.

But when she came to sentences rather than single words, the work slowed considerably.

Don Macario didn't know how to teach anyone a language, let alone a language that was not his own. He didn't know where one sentence ended and the next one began. He just knew the phrases you would need to get something done.

In Spanish, Elisabeth would ask him, "Wait, is that a suffix added on to the first word, like '-ing' or '-ed,'? You know, as in 'walking' or 'singing' or 'talking'?"

"I don't know, señorita!" Don Macario would answer. "That is just what they say."

"Well, perhaps that syllable is some sort of prefix starting off the next word, like 'in' or 're'?"

Don Macario threw up his hands. "I am doing the best I can, señorita, please do not ask me again!"

So Elisabeth tried to answer these questions herself, drawing slanted lines through breaks in the long phrases she had written. She prayed. She tried guessing. She kept listening to him say the same sentences again and again. After all, the Lord had put her here to bring the light of the gospel to these people. His triumph over their darkness would come quickly, she was certain. Her notebook on the Colorado language, which she discovered they themselves called 'Tsahfiki,' was slowly getting thicker and thicker.

When the Lord Destroys what He has Built

But things didn't always go as well as Elisabeth thought they would. For one thing, the Spanish Catholics didn't like the missionaries to be there, sharing a gospel witness about Jesus and how He died for our sins. The Catholics had been a religious presence in the area for many years. They liked the power they kept over the people by telling them that God was holding their sins over their heads. They assured the people that the priests could influence how the Lord parceled out blessing or forgiveness to them. This kept the Indian people in spiritual darkness.

For another thing, Elisabeth and her friends had been called upon to help a woman from one of the most influential families in the people group, the Quinones. Doreen, one of the missionaries, had told the woman that having another baby could be dangerous for her health. She already had eight or so, Elisabeth wasn't sure. Nevertheless, she was having another, and the four missionary women had been asked to help. They had assisted many other Spanish and Colorado women in child birth. They would help her again too. But this time, the woman had died. So had the baby. Now the Quinones family seemed somewhat distant. Would the missionaries be blamed for the deaths? And why hadn't the Lord kept the woman alive? After all, if He had shown this important family how strong He was, they might have been a bridge to bringing the gospel to all the people in the surrounding area. Elisabeth was afraid that their failure to save the woman had made the missionaries, and perhaps even the gospel, look weak.

She wrote another letter to Jim. "I find that I very soon get stale and fed up with life here. … I dawdle in quiet time, let my mind wander in prayer, and daydream when trying to study. Sometimes, I confess, after a long time on my knees and very little praying done … I call it quits, saying to myself, 'This isn't prayer. Might as well be up and doing something, even if it's only baking a cake or sharpening a pencil.'"[1] This was discouraging.

Unbeknownst to Elisabeth, there were more heartaches still to come.

Several months later, Elisabeth was sitting on her bed, a limp pillow behind her back, looking over her morning Bible reading. The early day was quiet and hinted at nothing more than language routine as usual.

"Think it not strange concerning the fiery trial which is to try you as though some strange thing happened unto you, but rejoice, inasmuch as ye are partakers in Christ's sufferings."(KJV)

---

1. Elisabeth Elliot, *These Strange Ashes* (New York: Harper & Row, 1975), p. 85.

She was musing over the verses in 1 Peter 4:12-13 when she heard gunshots outside. Shouts and the sound of horses trotting on the hard town mud quickly followed.

Elisabeth frowned. It wasn't too odd to hear gunshots. Sometimes the local men went hunting on the outskirts of the jungle close by.

Suddenly, her friend Doreen's voice burst into her reverie.

"They've killed Don Macario!" she shouted.

Other voices repeated the news.

"Macario has been shot! Macario is murdered!" The fateful chorus made its way throughout the town.

Elisabeth ran out of her room, her heart in her throat.

"What happened?!" she asked Lorenzo, Macario's Christian friend.

Lorenzo was dizzy with shock. "We were clearing the land over there," he began. He shook his head, still not believing what had happened.

"We were just chopping up some old limbs with our machetes," he said, breathless and shaky. "We were just working on Macario's land." He repeated himself several times, trying to convince himself of what he had seen with his own eyes but didn't want to believe.

"Well, who did it?" Elisabeth was pretty shaky herself.

"We were about to plant some banana trees there," Lorenzo pointed. "And some of the Quinones family rode up on their horses."

"The family of the girl who died?" Doreen exclaimed. "Oh no!"

"Yes," Lorenzo answered. "The Quinones brothers rode up and said that the land was theirs.

"So it was one of them?" Elisabeth asked.

"I didn't see for sure who did it," Lorenzo said. "But Don Macario told them the land was his."

"I heard them arguing," offered Doreen.

"Yes," Lorenzo finished. "Some of them got their guns out, but I didn't see who fired the shot. Some of the men were only Quinones hired hands."

"I'm going straight out there," Doreen announced.

"Oh no you're not," Elisabeth said. "Don't do a thing until we get the authorities.[2]

Later they wondered whether the murder had happened because of the jealousy over the missionaries' work. Rumor had it that one of the hires might have been paid by the Catholics to shoot Macario, since Macario had been helping Elisabeth with the language, but was not helping the Catholics.

Regardless of who did it, Elisabeth had lost the one man who could help her get the gospel to the Colorado Indians. What was God doing? She could not understand. It all seemed so confusing to her. He was the only man in the world who could speak both languages well. Didn't God care about this?

It was a tough test for Elisabeth's faith. But earlier, easier, tests that the Lord had given her had prepared

2. Ibid., p. 104.

her for this one. She didn't need to understand. She knew only to cultivate a spirit of acceptance. And in this case, she began to realize that when she humbly accepted what the Lord had sent, even when she saw absolutely nothing good come about, her acceptance opened the way to getting more of God Himself. In acceptance lies the way of knowing the Lord more deeply. As she grew in trust, she felt closer to the Lord.

Three days after Macario had died, Elisabeth received a letter from Jim asking her to come quickly. He told her he'd been given the freedom from the Lord to pursue marriage. Though Elisabeth wasn't sure exactly how Jim had come to the decision, it had something to do with how the Lord was teaching Jim in certain apparent failures in his own mission efforts. It was time to do something different.

He wanted to see her quickly in Quito. This was good news. There, he proposed to her. His only condition to actually getting married was that she had to learn Quichua first. Quichua was the language of the people group that Jim was working with at the other end of Ecuador.

On the way back to the Colorados from her visit with Jim, Elisabeth's heart sang. She was engaged to the man she loved, after four years of praying and waiting and hoping. She knew now that her time with the Colorados would be drawing to a close. She used the next few months to finish up the language research as efficiently as she could. Her extensive notebook, her charts of words and phrases filled out in her tightly knit cursive handwriting, and her box of neatly organized cards would provide a wonderful tool for someone else to take up. She thought her work would eventually make it possible for the Colorado Indians to have a Bible of their own. As for Elisabeth, she was glad to go. She headed to Quichua territory to begin learning the Quichua language. Never had she undertaken a language with more zeal.

But Don Macario's death was not to be the final time that Elisabeth's young faith would be stretched to the limit. Word of more bad news came a few days later from Doreen. Elisabeth's whole collection of cards, words, and sentences on the Colorado language had been lost from the top of a bus. Someone had stolen it. Nine months of meticulous research, nine months of her life, were simply gone! It was a big step backwards in getting the gospel to these people she had grown to love.

This was the final straw. Didn't the Lord want these people to get the gospel? Hadn't He called her to do this work? Was she mistaken in her call? Where had things gone wrong? She just didn't understand.

But Elisabeth felt she could only bow in humble adoration. "You are God, and I am not," she prayed. "You have the right to do what you want with your own work," she said. She accepted what she could not understand. And her heart was at rest.

Years later, she wrote a novel about her time with the Colorados. In the book, she fashioned the main character, a young woman, a missionary, who accidentally killed her first convert with an injection she had intended would cure his infection. It was a gritty story.

"It will keep people off the mission field," said many Christian leaders. "We cannot recommend this book. That's not the triumphant way that God works!"

"On the contrary," answered Ruth Bell Graham, the wife of famous evangelist Billy Graham. "The book will be a blessing. It will keep those people off the mission field who shouldn't be there anyway." She spoke wisdom to the critics. She knew that the Lord is not bound to work only in ways we can understand. Our faith is most beautiful when it perseveres in the darkness. She knew that missionaries on the field must be reminded that the Lord is working, despite what looks like success … or failure … to human eyes.

Yokefellows with a Vision

Elisabeth and Jim were married in Quito, Ecuador on October 8, 1953. Finally, Elisabeth could break down the dam that had held back her emotions for all those years she had waited patiently on God . . . and Jim! What a joy now to spend her life with the man she had loved for so long from a distance! Now they could serve the Lord together.

They spent a quiet week at an expensive hotel in Panama, enjoying a holiday from mission work as well as three warm showers a day. It was quite a luxury after the primitive conditions in which they usually worked.

They then made their way to Shandia, where Jim was rebuilding a mission outpost. This was the place he had suffered his setbacks. The building projects he had overseen for months and months—getting five buildings up and running for the mission team—had been washed down the river in a single night's flood. Like Elisabeth, Jim was also learning to trust the Lord's ways.

Shandia held its challenges for Elisabeth too. Until Jim could build them a house, they lived in a tent.

There were mornings when Elisabeth stepped off the air mattress that was their bed into standing water. Those jungle storms were fierce and sudden.

Soon, however, they moved to a beautifully scenic little place named Puyupungu. They had been invited by the chief to come and teach his people.

"Because of God, will you not stay?" he had asked. "We need you very much. I have—let's see—thirteen, fourteen, and another one, yes, fifteen children. No one has taught them. They want to learn to see paper. I have some orphans too in my house. Will you not come?"[1]

"We do not get along with the priests who have come before you," Chief Atanasio told Jim and Elisabeth. "I do not like the way they followed their God."

He had invited them to use the quarters that the Roman Catholic priests had used on their yearly visits to Chief Atanasio's village. Jim and Elisabeth called it "the convent." Cockroaches galore felt they had more right to the house than the Elliots, and the roof leaked.

"I do not think these priests will be back," Atanasio explained. "But my people want to hear more of the words of God."

It seemed a wide open door for the gospel. The chief was an intelligent man, and all his people respected him. If he told them to listen to the Bible, they would listen.

---

1. Elisabeth Elliot, *Through Gates of Splendor* (Peabody: Hendrickson, 1996), pp. 102-103.

It was also an opportunity to learn more Quichua, so that Elisabeth could help them get a Bible in their own language.

One morning, she was working with some of the Quichua Indian children in Puyupungu. From their perch high on the cliff beside the river where the Indians had made their settlement, she sat on a wooden box that had been used to carry flour, salt, rice, and beans to the missionaries—on the mission field, every item was repurposed for many other tasks. Off in the distance, she could see smoke rising from the world's most active volcano, El Sangay. From the top of this cliff, during the previous night, she had watched as fiery red boulders reeled downhill after being spewed from the mouth of the dark mountain. Truly, Puyupungu boasted the best view in the country.

"This is such a beautiful spot," she told them. "What does the name of your village mean?"

"'Puyu' is our river's name," the children told her. "It's like a 'cloud.'"

"Ok, right," Elisabeth remembered. "And 'pungu' means what?"

The children were stumped for a moment, figuring out their own language. "Well," said one, "It's like that," and he pointed toward the door of their little church house. But why would a village be named 'door'? 'Door' to the 'cloud'?

"Oh, I think I understand," replied Elisabeth. She pointed to her mouth. "Can 'pungu' also mean this?"

The children smiled and nodded. Now she was getting it. So their village was close to the mouth of the river. 'Puyupungu' meant 'mouth' (or 'door') of the river 'cloud.' She thought of her father. How grateful she was for the word-prone family the Lord had given her!

In her limited Quichua, she decided to try to share with them the story of Zaccheus. In halting but precise Quichua, she began.

"Zaccheus was a very small man." She dropped her hand to pretty close to the ground. The children giggled. She wondered why.

"Like us to you, Señora," said one little boy. "We are all like Zaccheus when we walk up to you."

She smiled with them and sighed. Here she was, hoping to give them light on what true repentance looked like. Instead, they were focused on how tall she was. Would it never end—how everyone seemed to notice her towering height?

"Well, Zaccheus met our Jesus," she went on, "and Jesus forgave his sins. Remember, children, that Jesus was sent to earth to die for our sins."

"And when He forgave Zaccheus, Zaccheus was so captured by Jesus' love for him that he immediately wanted to make right the ugly things he had done to others."

"Lord, please give them understanding," Elisabeth prayed as she taught. She had so warmed into the story, that she had not noticed Chief Atanasio standing at the edge of the group, leaned in and listening close.

When the story was complete and the children had scattered, the chief approached her with his slow dignity.

"Señora Elliot," he said, "I am perhaps too old to learn these words that you are telling my children." His eyes were soft and serious.

"It gives my heart hope that you and Señor Jim came to our village. You are like the mouth of God to us," he continued. He spoke with an intent frown.

"I am very old. Perhaps too old to understand well. But it seems to me your words are true. I will die in your words."[2]

Elisabeth and Jim rejoiced. The power of the gospel could not be stopped by flood or failure or fearful obstacles. They were learning that they could rejoice when days were good and embrace the days that were bad. "In acceptance lieth peace," they knew, because God is still in control.

"How beautiful on the mountains are the feet of those who bring good news, who proclaim peace, who bring good tidings, who proclaim salvation, who say to Zion, 'Your God reigns!'" (Isaiah 52:7 NIV).

2. Ibid., p. 103.

New Horizons

The days were drawing close to Christmas, and Elisabeth was hopeful of a letter from her folks back home. She had tuned her ears to hear the difference between the low rumble of their neighbor the volcano, the melodious bustle of the river at the foot of the cliff, and the distant hum of the little Piper Cruiser plane that their friend Nate Saint flew to bring their weekly supplies. They had brought in most of their stuff so far by wobbly canoes that threatened to dump their precious cargo into the whirling rapids that had to be navigated on the way to Puyupungu. Now that they had an airstrip, Nate could land for emergencies or simply drop their supplies by air.

On Nate's first visit, the villagers ran to the airstrip. They waved an eager greeting to the bright plane, buzzing like a bee above their heads.

"He's throwing it! He's throwing it! He's throwing it!"[1] she heard Chief Atanasio shouting at the top of his lungs.

1. Elisabeth Elliot to folks, December 5, 1953, Folder 1, Box 4, Collection 278, Papers of Elisabeth Howard Elliot, Archives of the Billy Graham Center, Wheaton, Illinois..

"Stand clear, everyone!" Jim called out in Quichua. "Watch out you don't get hit!"

A cheerful orange parachute sailed gracefully out of the plane and landed with a promising thud at their feet. Elisabeth was thrilled. From the bundle, she drew out fresh beef and vegetables and powdered milk and medicine, sent for their needs by Marj, Nate's wife, who manned the radio at the plane base. And the mail had come too. There were letters from her family! Her hands flew to open her mother's letter.

"My dear daughter," it began. "I hope you do not grow weary of these weekly screeds that I send to you." Elisabeth laughed at that. However could she grow tired of hearing news of her dear family?

"We are settling into the holidays. Your brother Tom will sing in this year's *Messiah*. Your little brother Jim is coming home from college for Thanksgiving and Christmas break, though he may travel through a blizzard to get here—we are having that kind of weather," her mother continued. "And I have laid out the English thorn and fine China."

From her mom's homey description, Elisabeth could almost smell the turkey in the oven.

"I am reading through Amy Carmichael's biography, since you have gained so much from her life," the letter went on. "I'm enjoying every moment of it." Then her mom asked some questions.

"Betty, dear, are you losing weight? You look so thin in the photos you sent. And your wedding photos were wonderful to behold. Who was the little tot in galoshes? And just who was that policeman fellow, standing outside? Enclosed is an article from your father about mountain climbing," the letter drew to a close, decorated with lots of exclamation marks and underlines.

Elisabeth smiled. Her mother never failed to love her children and take a lively interest in their activities, no matter how spread out the family became.

She hurried to dash off an answer in the hope that the folks back home would get it in time for Christmas.

> *Dearest folks,*
>
> *Jim is doing a beautiful job making cabinets for me in the kitchen. My, he surely knows how." Elisabeth's reports of her new husband were glowing. "He's making them from old canoes which the Indians had discarded, and some boards we brought with us.*
>
> *No, Mother, we do not get tired of 'these weekly screeds.' Don't know what we'd do without them. We always look forward to them more than anything, and it is such a comfort to know that there's always at least one in every batch of mail.*[2]

Elisabeth continued, describing their work with the Indians and remarking on all the family news.

> *You spoke of enjoying Amy Carmichael's biography, Mother. Jim and I are reading a chapter every night before we go to sleep, and find it very stimulating. She seemed a very balanced girl, didn't she?*[3]

2. Ibid.
3. Ibid.

She assured her mother she had no idea who the policeman was, or who the tot in galoshes was. Then, she tried to calm her mother's worries.

> *I have not lost a single pound since you saw me; my clothes all fit me just the same, and I weigh 126, the same I've weighed for the last twelve years.*[4]

Finally she closed her letter, her heart brimful.

> *I can't realize Christmas is only three weeks from today. I will be thinking of you all, and rejoicing with you, for there's nothing like a Christmas at Birdsong! I can ask nothing more than what the Lord has given me, in showing me His will, leading me, and giving me Jim. I am happier than I've ever been in my life, and grateful to God. ...*
>
> *Loving you all,*
> *Betty*[5]

The future was bright. Though Elisabeth did not know it all yet, the new year, 1954, would bring new blessings to the Jim Elliot family. They would return to Shandia to continue the work there. She and Jim would learn that they were expecting a child. And the Lord would begin to lay a pioneer work on the hearts of Nate Saint, Jim Elliot, and three other missionary men in Ecuador. They began learning about a tribe deep in the heart of the jungle, a fierce tribe, a tribe of killers, a tribe with whom no white man had ever had dealings and lived to tell about it: the Aucas. Together, the men would brainstorm about how to reach these people—people

4. Ibid.
5. Ibid.

who lived far beyond the mission outposts they knew so far. Surely the Lord had it in mind that these isolated, primitive peoples should hear the good news of Jesus.

Operation Auca

The year of 1954 came and went, and soon the Elliot family entered another new phase of life. February, 1955, little Valerie was born into the Elliot home. Elisabeth and Jim could hardly contain their joy over the merry little wisp of a girl the Lord had given them.

Also, during the months of 1955, their good friend Nate began to make trips out deep into the jungle, scouting the area for Auca settlements. Jim and their buddy Ed were elated when Nate spotted some clearings scattered with thatched roof houses. The jungle was so huge and so thick that when the little plane suddenly happened upon a little clearing of huts, it was a miracle. Truly, the world of flight and technology had opened up the ends of the earth to the gospel! The naked Indians looked up at them curiously, but showed no fear at the sight of the yellow plane. They didn't seem that impressed that men could fly. Nate's reports encouraged the other missionary men.

By now, a few of the five men began meeting, spreading out a map of the jungle on the floor in the Saints' living room at Shell Mera to talk and plan.

The five men lived about twenty minutes or so flight from each other. Shell Mera was the mission hub—a leftover oil base built by white men once there drilling the rich oil reserves. From Shell Mera, Marj looked after everyone else by radio contact. Nate parked his airplane there when not in use. Pete and Olive Fleming moved into Puyupungu to take up the ministry where the Elliots had left off, baptizing many converted Indians. Roger Youderian, once a paratrooper who saw action at the Battle of the Bulge during World War II, and his wife Barbara worked with the Jivaro Indians quite a bit further south. The Jivaros were famous for the shrunken heads of victims they took in battle. The Youderians only heard of the Auca plan later in the game, but Roger was immediately up for it.

Ed and Marilou McCully and and their two little boys moved into Arajuno. Though they would work with the hundred or so Quichua Indians who lived near the camp, theirs was the station closest to Auca territory. So the Quichua Indians there gave them up-to-date reports of the latest dreadful things Aucas were doing. From the journals of the men and from Elisabeth's writing, we can piece together what their conversations must have been like.

"I've located a couple of settlements now within fifteen flight minutes of Arajuno," Nate told the men one night.

"We've told the Quichuas around our stations to keep quiet about what we're doing," Pete added. "If any local parties who don't care about the Indians hear our plans, they will only want to invade with guns, due to their fear of the Aucas."

"Yes, we've got to keep this under wraps," said Jim. "The Indians have known only hostile contact from white men."

"Aucas speared three employees of the oil company in 1942, then another eight men in 1943," Ed put in. "Though gifts of shirts, machetes, magazines, and bottles were left for them, there was really no progress made in forming friendly relations."

"I think that the Aucas made a return on the gifts with one of their baskets made of vines," Ed continued. "But the old men who once explored the jungle for rubber, gold, and oil say that peaceful contact is impossible."

"That's because the Aucas knew they carried guns," conjectured Jim. "And they knew that guns meant death for them."

"Are they killers by nature?" the men wondered. "Or do they kill simply when they are in the act of stealing things from the settlements? Or do they kill because many of them have been killed by white men and they consider us enemies?" No one knew for sure.

"The Quichuas are always on the lookout for signs of Auca presence around our station," Ed said. "Whenever they see grass that is flattened or footprints around the house, they are sure that Aucas have been spying on us."

"We try to keep a pistol handy around our house," Ed continued. "And we keep an electric fence up and buzzing, so that we are alerted if anyone comes within spear-throwing distance of the house.

"But if we ever make a venture into Auca territory, I think we should go unarmed. They will never believe our friendly intentions if we carry guns."

"Agreed," answered Jim. "We must promise each other that if we make contact, we'll not use guns, even in self-defense, unless it's some sort of terrible emergency. For myself," Jim continued, "... if that's the way God wants it to be, I'm ready to die for the salvation of the Aucas."

"After all," chimed in Nate, "we're ready for heaven and they're not."[1]

"Agreed," they all said. "No guns."

It seemed to the men that God was opening the door for friendly contact to be made with the savage tribe. In his living room, Nate had practiced and perfected a most accurate method in his plane for sending down supplies and gifts without landing. He first had the idea by twirling a pencil from a string, round and round in a circle until centrifugal force kept the pencil almost still at the bottom of the string, even while the top of the string kept twirling widely from his extended finger. If he could

---

1. Elisabeth Elliot, *Through Gates of Splendor* (Peabody: Hendrickson, 1996), p. 173.

get this to work from a plane, it meant that a person on the ground wouldn't need to run around trying to catch a dangling line while the plane was moving at forty or so miles per hour. From the friendly yellow wings hovering hundreds of feet above the village, he could drop a basket on the line and begin to fly in a circle. Once the plane stabilized into a steady turn, the line would eventually hang almost motionless. In this way, they could get gifts to the Indians in a very user-friendly way without putting their own lives at risk by landing before friendly contact was established. Plus, the Aucas might tie something into the basket to send back up to the missionaries.

Then the Lord provided something even more helpful. Word came to Jim and Elisabeth that an Auca woman was close by. She had escaped from her tribe and was living with some neighboring Quichuas. Her name was Dayuma and she was friendly.

"What an answer to prayer!" Elisabeth thought. "Now, Jim and I can meet her and learn some Auca words and phrases so that we can make friendly conversation with them when we meet."

While Nate began making gift drops over the Auca settlements, Jim and Elisabeth began learning the Auca language from Dayuma.

"How do you say, 'I like you?'" they asked her.

"Biti miti punimupa," she answered. "It also means 'I want to be your friend.'"

"What about something like 'let's get together'?" Jim asked.

"*Biti winki pungi amupa*," Dayuma said.

"How do you say, 'what is your name'?" Jim asked in Quichua.

"*Awum irimi*," Dayuma answered in Auca.[2]

Nate dropped the Aucas an aluminum pot and some colorful buttons—for decoration and not for sewing onto clothes. Remember, they wore no clothes. He dropped them some pretty ribbons and some rock salt—would they pick up on what it was for? Everything was geared to show the savages that the white men had peaceful, loving intentions.

Christmas came, and the missionaries met together, celebrated and counted the cost of a try with the Aucas.

Nate wrote in his journal, "As we weigh the future and seek the will of God, does it seem right that we should hazard our lives for just a few savages?

"May God help us to judge ourselves by the eternities that separate the Aucas from a comprehension of Christmas and Him, who, though he was rich, yet for our sakes became poor ...."[3]

Elisabeth wrote home to her mother to get her to pray for the coming contact. She knew it would be soon. The men felt that the Lord was opening the way to land the plane in Auca territory, on a strip of sand by the Curaray River they had dubbed "Palm Beach."

---

2. Ibid., pp. 114-115.
3. Ibid., pp. 177-178.

Top Secret
Shandia, Jan. 2, 1956

Dearest Mother,

The fellows plan to take off on Wednesday for the Auca trip, Lord willing. ... I suppose Marj will have some sort of code worked out [to let the wives know how things are going over the radio without unsympathetic listeners being able to listen in].

Did I tell you that on the flights they have made the Aucas have returned their gifts. ... It certainly is fantastic and thrilling to actually handle feather head-dresses made by a tribe of people totally untouched by civilization ....

The fellows will wear the feather headdresses on the trip, and Nate has already dropped to them (the Aucas) two or three sets of big portrait photographs of the members of the party, so that if they encounter the Aucas, they will be recognized (we hope!) .... [4]

The Indians had also managed to get several other gifts tucked into the basket before it was hoisted back up. The basket flew back to Shell Mera in the wake of Nate's plane carrying two squirrels, some bracelets, some packets of peanuts, and a parrot (which was quickly adopted by Nate's son, little Stevie). Surely this tribe understood and welcomed their friendly overtures!

Only once has a lance been in sight when they have flown over, and that was quickly hidden, so perhaps they are

---

4. Elisabeth Elliot to Folks, January 2, 1956, Folder 4, Box 4, Collection 278, Papers of Elisabeth Howard Elliot, Archives of the Billy Graham Center, Wheaton, Illinois.

showing their friendliness that way. It is all very intriguing and fascinating, and we are wild to know what their reactions to all the drops have been.

I am at perfect peace about Jim's going. I hope you will not worry. The Lord has given direction, and confidence. We are in His keeping, and want Him to be glorified.

With ever so much love,

Betty[5]

---

5. Ibid.

Taking Christmas to the Savages

The next day, the men had taken off with Nate in the yellow plane. Jim had kissed his Betty goodbye and shouldered his pack.

"Betty, darling, if I don't come back," he looked at her meaningfully, "teach the believers." And then he was off. He didn't look back. She stood there wondering, "Will I ever see him coming back up this path?

Elisabeth busied herself with the care of now ten-month-old Valerie and kept in touch with the other wives. She and Marj and Marilou and the other women agreed that they were at one with their husbands in supporting the mission. Now they could only wait and pray as the men set up camp on the beach, deep in Auca territory.

Out in the jungle, the men hoisted boards up to the limbs of an enormous tree and crafted themselves a treehouse. Thirty five feet up, they felt safe to sleep at night without fear of an attack.

Once they built safe shelter, they waited on a visit from their new neighbors. The wait was long. Jim went fishing, caught a catfish and roasted it over the fire. Roger and Nate threw termites' nests on the fire to create a smoke that would chase the millions of gnats away.

The men went exploring and saw puma and tapir tracks. They drank lemonade. They went swimming. Submerged in the water, to keep cool and away from bugs, they read books and magazines. They took pictures. They wrote in their journals. They made jokes about the books, and the flies, and the heat. Then Jim would get the loudspeaker and shout Auca phrases out into the jungle.

"Come to the Curaray. We want to be your friends. We like you!"

Every day, they wrote letters to their wives and contacted them by radio to give them detailed reports. Elisabeth and her friends were grateful for every word. So far, so good.

Several times, the men felt eyes watching them. But no one showed up.

Finally, four days after they'd landed, three Aucas stepped into their camp. The man had round wooden plugs stuffed through his earlobes. Two women lagged behind, one old and one young. The young one had plugs in her earlobes too, but the only other clothing any of them wore were strings around their waists.

"*Puinanis!*" the men called in unison. "Welcome!"

The three Aucas seemed friendly. The missionaries offered them rubber bands, balloons, and a yo-yo, then some hamburgers and lemonade. Then they offered the man a shirt and took him for a ride in the airplane. The man laughed and shouted. This first visit looked like it was a success.

Sunday, Pete and Nate went back for a stop at Shell Mera to restock some of their supplies. Marj, Marilou, and Olive were waiting.

"Our three visitors left Saturday morning and we haven't seen them again, but it was a very good first contact." Pete's spirits were high. "I think we'll meet the rest of the group very soon."

As he climbed back into the airplane, he looked back at the wives. "So long, girls. Pray. I believe today's the day."[1]

And yes, it was the day. At noon, the men radioed back to the wives, excited.

"There's a group of about ten on their way here right now," Nate reported.

"Looks like they'll be here for the Sunday afternoon service. We'll call you back at 4:30," he promised.

At 4:30, the women gathered around the radios, listening in from both Shell Mera and Arajuno. They were eager to hear from their men. Had the Indians come? Did they have a good visit? Had they been invited into the thatched roof houses as friends?

But 4:30 came, and went. The radio was silent. The wives reassured each other. Perhaps their watches were

---

1. Elisabeth Elliot, *Through Gates of Splendor* (Peabody: Hendrickson, 1996), p. 196.

slow. Or perhaps the men were deep in conversation with their new Auca friends.

But by the next morning, there was still no word. They told a fellow missionary.

"I'm flying in for a look," he said.

What he saw shook him. He found Nate's plane on the beach, stripped of its happy yellow fabric. None of the men could be seen.

"It looks bad, girls," he radioed back to the station.

Elisabeth hurried to Shell Mera to gather with the other four women. "Lord, you promised that when we passed through the waters, they will not overflow us," she prayed. "Be with us, Lord. Please don't let the waters overflow."

Through Gates of Splendor

The January 30, 1956 issue of LIFE magazine cost twenty cents. On its cover were headlines about an interview with Harry S. Truman, the United States president at the end of World War II, and with Henry Ford's grandson about the Ford Motor Company. Truman discussed his memories of the Marshall Plan, and the intent to restore Europe after the war, and his widely criticized support of the birth of the state of Israel. Letters to the editor discussed Russia and whether we should come out strong against the communists or share cultural exchanges with them. Other letters argued about whether soldiers should dance at military functions and whether theaters should show plays and movies that mentioned gambling and drugs. Readers wrote in with opinions about Ghandi and the riots in India. Eleanor Roosevelt and Winston Churchill made minor headlines. Flashy full page ads promoted movie stars, boasted of the benefits of washing machines, cars, dental check-ups and milk.

At its height, LIFE magazine circulated to thirteen and a half million American homes every week.

But on page ten of this issue, there is a stark black and white photo of five young women sitting around a kitchen table. It takes up almost the entire width of the over-sized, two-page spread. There are half-eaten sandwiches on the plates in front of them, and toddlers wiggling in their laps and on their shoulders. They listen to a man with his back to the camera. They look serious and focused on what the man is saying. The man is telling them about the search party that found the dead bodies of their five husbands. The Aucas had speared them, all of them, to death. The man has just told them that they are now widows.

On the same page is a photo of the Auca man who visited the men on the beach that Friday before the fateful day. He is looking into the camera, a machete behind him given to him by the missionaries, and a wooden model of the Piper Cruiser over his shoulder. The headline reads, *"'Go Ye and Preach the Gospel' Five Do and Die."*

Yes, it had been the day all right.

Using the journals of the men, the LIFE magazine photographer, Cornell Capa, wrote the story of the deaths. The pages show photos of the five men, smiling into the camera, not yet knowing that they would yield their lives for the spread of the good news of Jesus. Yet all of them had declared that they were willing.

The wives were willing too. Though the husbands had sacrificed their lives, the wives had sacrificed men they dearly loved. They gave up having a whole family. They gave up the security of having a husband. Now all of them would need to figure out how to do life on their own. Four of them had small children. Now they would need to be mommy and daddy to these youngsters. But they had known that death might be a possibility, and they had supported their husbands' decisions. Jesus was worthy of anything and everything they could give.

Within days, the story of their sacrifice had circled around the world. People were amazed, in an era of peace and prosperity, that Christians were still willing to pursue something bigger than money or the American dream. They were amazed that primitive tribes like the Aucas still existed—people who knew nothing about the outside world and were locked in their own dark lives of murder and superstition. They were most amazed that Christians could love Jesus as much as these men and their wives did, to try to reach these killers.

Elisabeth took comfort in the writings of her favorite missionary again.

Hast thou no scar?
No hidden scar on foot, or side, or hand?
I hear thee sung as mighty in the land,
I hear them hail thy bright ascendant star,
Hast thou no scar?

Hast thou no wound?
Yet I was wounded by the archers, spent,
Leaned Me against a tree to die; and rent

> By ravening beasts that compassed Me, I swooned:
> Hast thou no wound?
>
> No wound, no scar?
> Yet, as the Master shall the servant be,
> And, pierced are the feet that follow Me;
> But thine are whole: can he have followed far
> Who has no wound nor scar?
>
> Amy Carmichael

Now Elisabeth had a deep wound, a scar that would be on her heart for the rest of her life. It came from following her Master. Yet she was not bitter toward the Aucas. They didn't know better. For they did not yet know her precious Jesus.

Elisabeth went back to Shandia with Olive Fleming, one of the other widows, and carried on with the work there. After all, those were the final instructions that her beloved Jim had given her. She felt the Lord would have it that way too.

Do the Next Thing

The Lord had other duties for Elisabeth as well.

"Come to New York with me," insisted her new friend Cornell Capa. "One of your fellow missionaries was writing a book about your husbands, but the publishers are not sure about it. I told them to talk to you."

"You need to ask Betty Elliot," Cornell had instructed them. "She's a good writer, and she can help you out."

Mr Capa was not a believer, but the story of the five men had struck a deep chord in his heart when he had come to the jungle reporting for LIFE magazine. Elisabeth hoped for a chance to tell him about Jesus. So when the publishers contacted her, she agreed to the trip.

When she arrived in New York, notable people from all over the country wanted to meet her. Even though she was fresh from the jungle, Elisabeth impressed all of them with the graceful ease she had when speaking with everyone from dignitaries like the mayor and ambassadors from various countries' embassies, to pushy reporters and publishers.

The media gurus from Harper and Row Publishers sat her down at a typewriter.

"Write something," they instructed her.

"What do you want me to write?" she asked.

"Write whatever you want," they suggested.

"Alright," she replied. "I'll write about a day on a jungle trail with an Auca Indian." She clacked out a few thoughtful sentences until they became a paragraph. Then she looked up. The publisher was leaning close by, reading over her shoulder as she worked. He yanked the paper out of the typewriter and scanned it.

"This speaks!" he said. He was enthusiastic.

Elisabeth smiled, still in the dark.

"Now we can tell you why we really wanted you to come to New York," he said. "We need you to write this book! Cornell assured us that you were the one we would want."

"Really?" She was not expecting this.

Well, hadn't the Lord been preparing her all along with this love of words that she had? She agreed to the project.

Back in Shandia, little Valerie and the work with the Quichuas kept her busy. Somehow, she managed to fit in writing a book. Elisabeth completed the story with her fatherless child in her arms. Under her pen, the testimony of the five men and their love for the Lord sang out with courage and clarity.

When she mailed her final manuscript in to the publisher, the pages were yellowed and thin and had bug stains on them. But when the pages became a book, the story became an overnight sensation. *Through Gates of Splendor* was the title she gave it, after the hymn the five men sang together on the beach the morning they launched Operation Auca.

> We rest on Thee, our Shield and our Defender!
> Thine is the battle, Thine shall be the praise;
> When passing through the gates of pearly splendor,
> Victors, we rest with Thee, through endless days.
>
> Edith Cherry

Newspapers and magazines heralded her book. Book reviews called her writing "simple, restrained, and forthright." Elisabeth wrote with dignity and dramatic force, they said. It was one of the greatest missionary accounts ever written.

"Nothing in modern literature has dramatized so strikingly the collision of old and new, of faith and primitive superstition, as *Through Gates of Splendor*, the saga of the five young missionary martyrs, who in their small plane, were the first in centuries to penetrate the dread land of the Auca Indian, with the Christian gospel, only to be slain," wrote a reviewer. "Yet, transcending the tragedy of this amazing Christian adventure ... was the five missionaries' unquenchable faith in the ultimate purpose of God and their joyous devotion to Christ."[1]

The word Auca became a household word in America. Young people read the book and gave their hearts to Christ. Others gave their lives to spread the gospel

---

1. Various newspaper clippings, Folder 1, Box 1, Collection 278, Papers of Elisabeth Howard Elliot, Archives of the Billy Graham Center, Wheaton, Illinois.

on distant mission fields. The Lord used the book in powerful ways. There are missionaries right now serving in Africa and South America and countries throughout the world because of the way God spoke to them through Elisabeth's story of Jim and Nate and their three friends.

And Elisabeth, still tucked away in a remote corner of the jungle, became a national figure without realizing it. She had no idea her name was becoming known all over the world. She counted herself as very obscure. And though she still felt a huge hole that Jim's love had once filled, and Valerie and she were alone in the world, she had determined to accept her situation as from God. Valerie's toddler antics kept her amused, and the mission work kept her hands full.

Elisabeth helped her little daughter with her prayers one night.

"Dear Lord, thank you for your love," Elisabeth led out.

"Dear Lord, thank you for my love,"[2] Valerie followed—sort of.

"No, Valerie, when we pray, we're talking to the Lord Jesus," Elisabeth corrected gently. "We thank Him for His love."

"But He doesn't talk," Valerie protested.

"No, not so we can hear Him with our ears," Elisabeth explained.

"Does my Daddy talk?" Valerie questioned.

---

2. Elisabeth Elliot to Folks, February 11, 1958, Folder 6, Box 4, Collection 278, Papers of Elisabeth Howard Elliot, Archives of the Billy Graham Center, Wheaton, Illinois.

"Yes, he talks to Jesus."[3]

"Does he talk to our friends? Does he talk to you?"

Elisabeth's heart ached with the effort of trying to balance hard life questions with her daughter's innocence. There were still weeks on end that she dreamed of Jim almost every night. At the same time, she felt less attached to the world; she enjoyed Valerie but felt she did not possess her—she couldn't feel that she really owned anything. And she found herself surprisingly free from fear and worry—she, who once was called a "worry-wort" by her husband. She had one foot in heaven now, and the things of earth were growing strangely dimmer by the day.

"I am thirty-one, as of three weeks ago," she wrote a good friend. "Wish I were eighty-one."[4] She didn't really want to live many more years with as much sorrow as the future appeared to hold.

"I look forward with great longing to being at Home," she went on. "No place on earth will ever be home again without Jim. God has to use severe methods, to cause us to see all in His arms."[5]

Once you come face to face with death, she realized, the world loses its grip on your heart. For Elisabeth, just wanted to figure out how the Lord wanted her to live out the rest of her days. Her only question was

3. Ibid.
4. Elisabeth Elliot to Carol Smith Graham, January 14, 1958, Folder 2, Box 1, Collection 278, Papers of Elisabeth Howard Elliot, Archives of the Billy Graham Center, Wheaton, Illinois.
5. Ibid.

what she should do next, since she was one of the ones still living. Then she came across another poem which helped her to know.

At an old English parsonage down by the sea,
there came in the twilight a message to me.
Its quaint Saxon legend deeply engraven
that, as it seems to me, teaching from heaven.
And all through the hours the quiet words ring,
like a low inspiration, 'Do the next thing.'

Many a questioning, many a fear,
many a doubt hath its quieting here.
Moment by moment, let down from heaven,
time, opportunity, guidance are given.
Fear not tomorrow, child of the King,
trust that with Jesus, do the next thing.

Do it immediately, do it with prayer,
do it reliantly, casting all care.
Do it with reverence, tracing His hand,
who placed it before thee with earnest command.
Stayed on omnipotence, safe 'neath His wing,
leave all resultings, do the next thing.

Looking to Jesus, ever serener,
working or suffering be thy demeanor,
in His dear presence, the rest of His calm,
the light of His countenance, be thy psalm.
Do the next thing.
                    (Source unknown)

Elisabeth need only to find what the next thing was.

The Savage, my Kinsman

The answer arrived in a manner Elisabeth would never have been able to guess. It was two years after Jim's death. Operation Auca had been abandoned, and the missionaries still willing to work at the other mission stations had returned to work. She had been desperately trying to do by herself all that she and Jim had once done together. It was hard. Yet, she felt she should pray, "Lord, if there's anything you want me to do about the Aucas, I'm available."

And then one day, two Quichuas found her visiting at the home of a missionary friend on an errand that she hadn't really wanted to do. It turned out to be a divine appointment.

"Señora, we left our houses when the sun was over there," they pointed to a mountain due east. "Now the sun is here," they pointed straight up. "There are two Auca women at our settlement. They have escaped from their tribe. Do you want to talk with them?"

Elisabeth squinted into the sun. Judging by its place, she guessed they had walked about six hours to reach her.

"We must return soon, señora," they urged. "We must be back at our village before the sun goes there," they looked west. "Do you want to come with us or no?"

She conferred with the missionary about Valerie's care and agreed to go. It seemed a clear answer to her prayer.

On the way down the path, Elisabeth's Quichua companions provided a running commentary on every suspicious mark on the trail.

"Look, the grass is flat," they hissed nervously to each other, "See they lie there, then they will spear us!"

"Look! A broken twig!" they jumped. "That's their sign. They know which way we go and they signal each other."[1] It seemed to Elisabeth that they imagined new dangers with each step. Fear of the Auca darkened their way.

Yet Elisabeth walked with a spring in her step. This was the next thing her heavenly Father had given her to do. She only needed to follow, a step at a time. It didn't take the fact that they arrived at their destination unspeared to give her heart peace.

Elisabeth met the two women there and accompanied them back to her station by plane. They lived with her for two years. Once with the Auca women, Elisabeth set her focus on learning all she could about this tribe. These women, Mintaka and Mankamu, along with their friend Dayuma, taught her much about the language. Could they be the missionaries' ticket into the tribe

---

1. Elisabeth Elliot, *"Serenity,"* CD Lars Gren Collection.

of killers? But after two years, the women had their own ideas about their future plans. They pointed to a jungle tree. "When the palm fruit ripens, we will go back to our homes," they told Elisabeth. "And we want you to come with us."

"Will they kill me too?" Elisabeth asked them. She had her hesitations.

"No, you are a woman!" the women said.

"Will I be safe?" she asked. "Will my daughter be safe?"

They laughed and reassured her. But how could she be assured about people who killed so easily?

In time, Elisabeth, Valerie, and Rachel Saint, Nate's sister, went to live with the tribe. They learned that the term "Auca" was only the name the Quichuas had given them to label them as wild, naked savages—they called themselves the Waorani. The Waorani called Elisabeth "Gikari," or Woodpecker. Elisabeth wryly wondered what gave them that idea.

She and Valerie "moved" into a house that had no walls, just like those of the Waorani. They ate barbecued monkey and wild pig, just like the Waorani. They swam and bathed in the Curaray River alongside the Waorani … and snakes. It was not a time to be cowardly.

In the outside world, everyone was still paying attention to Elisabeth's remote activities. A young woman goes to live with the savages who killed her husband? Surely not! And with her little girl! How would she manage? How could she risk their lives like that? Back home in the States, people were still riveted by the story of Elisabeth's life-sacrificing choices.

Meanwhile, the hard questions that Valerie posed to her mom became even harder. But Elisabeth didn't hold to the idea of coddling children or being too protective.

"Is that my daddy?"[2] She scampered up to her mom one day holding hands with a smiling brown man. They'd just returned from a jungle jaunt.

"No, Valerie," Elisabeth replied. "That's one of the men who killed your father."

Elisabeth just never could mince words.

Amazingly, the Lord began softening the hearts of the Waorani people. Dayuma explained to Elisabeth and Rachel their traditional view of death.

"My grandfather told me that there were two deaths," Dayuma told them one day. "The first time you die, your bones will rot but your soul will walk along a trail up to the sky."

"When you get half way there, you will see a big worm, and you won't be able to get by it," she continued. "Being afraid, you will return. That is what my grandfather told me."

"So I asked my grandfather what would happen if I return. He told me I would become a termite!" Dayuma looked horrified, remembering it.

"Then I asked him what would happen to me after I had become a termite. He told me I would just die,

---

2. Elisabeth Elliot, *The Savage My Kinsman* (Ann Arbor: Servant Publications, 1981) p. 65.

my soul would die, and that is the end." To a Waorani, what happens to the body after death was a subject filled with awe and fear. So the story of Jesus and his death and resurrection into heaven was amazing to them. It was almost too good to be true. Elisabeth worked furiously to get their language transcribed into recognizable signs and letters in preparation for a future Bible translation for the tribe, while Rachel shared orally as best she could.

"So what will you tell your son about death now?" Rachel asked Dayuma one day. This Waorani woman had been under the teaching of the gospel by the two missionaries for months by then.

"Now I will tell him that if he dies first and goes to God's house in heaven, I will come later and see him again. And if I die first, I will go to heaven, and he will come later, and I will see him again. There will be no fear, just good. That is the way it was with Jesus. And it is so with you and with me if we believe God's carvings."[3]

Others in the tribe also settled down and listened to the message. In time, even some of the men who had participated in the spearings of the five missionaries said they wanted to "follow God's trail" and "believe in His carvings." Elisabeth was happy to see these signs of spiritual hunger, but she also longed to see the gospel overcome their tendency to be cruel and to laugh at

3. Fred Jarvis, "With the Widows in Auca Land," Christian Life, May 1958, Folder 1, Box 1, Collection 278, Papers of Elisabeth Howard Elliot, Archives of the Billy Graham Center, Wheaton, Illinois.

things that hurt others. Because of this, Elisabeth often questioned how effective her time with the Waoranis was from an eternal perspective. Explaining and living out the gospel with the Waorani tribe gave her new things to do all the time—the next things.

Doing the Next Thing
Back Home

Elisabeth lived for almost two years with the tribe. Eventually, she felt that she needed to get Valerie back to the States for her education. It had grown to be quite the challenge for eight-year-old Valerie to concentrate on reading, writing, and arithmetic when Indian children were constantly giggling at her, experimenting with her crayons, trimming things with her scissors, and peering into the window or over her shoulder. After all, she had to do school and many of them did not!

So Elisabeth moved back to the states in 1963. With the royalties from the sales of her books, she built a house for Valerie and her in Franconia, New Hampshire. Franconia was a small town surrounded by green woods and wildlife. The town was turning into a resort area, and people flocked to see the home next door to Elisabeth's, where the poet Robert Frost had once lived. She was excited to live so close to a fellow writer's house. By now, she'd written the story of the missionaries' martyrdom, the story of her time with the Waorani, and she had compiled Jim's journal entries into a volume that would one day acquaint Valerie with her beloved father. People were asking for more.

Young Valerie had some adjustments to make, living back in the States when all she'd known was the jungle. For starters, people wore clothes here. They ate with forks and knives. And they all spoke only English. This was hard when Valerie was so fluent in the languages of her Indian friends.

So Elisabeth tried to help Valerie feel more at home. Growing up with Elisabeth as a mom was an adventure! She allowed Valerie to have a lot of pets, not only a long succession of dogs and cats, but also a woodchuck, an otter, and a monkey who made himself a complete nuisance. They eventually had to get rid of him!

One autumn evening, Elisabeth coaxed a little fire into warming the tiny parlor in their new home. Outside the window, a porcupine trundled down the driveway and a woodchuck scuttled home before twilight. And inside by the front door, Zip, their dog, put his paw over Chuckles, so that their rotund pet groundhog would quit biting at Zip's ears and fur and climbing up on his back to slide down the other side.

Elisabeth chose a book that she and Valerie would read together that night. They settled in on the sofa with mugs of hot chocolate on the table beside their propped-up, socked feet.

"Here's one we can read for a while," she told her daughter. "It's called *Little House in the Big Woods*. I think you will like it."

That night, they made their way through tales of Ma and her churn-dash whipping silky milk into golden butter, Jack the brindle bulldog chasing the wolves away, the aunts with their petticoats and corset strings dancing across grandpa's wood floor, and Pa with his fiddle and twinkling blue eyes, singing to the girls every evening.

"I love this book, Mama!" Valerie cried. "Everything Laura Ingalls writes about is so cozy."

"Yes," said Elisabeth. "It was one of my favorites when I was your age."

"The family seems so happy together," observed Valerie. "It feels warm, somehow."

"What do you think makes them so happy?" Elisabeth liked to ask questions that made her daughter think. "What is the most important thing in that home?" She was expecting Valerie to answer "love."

"A daddy!" Valerie rejoined. "That's what they have."

Elisabeth smiled. "God is like a daddy to you, you know, now that you've lost your daddy," She paused, thinking through her words carefully. "He is letting us get to know His love better, by being a father to us in our loneliness, Valerie. He will love us and take care of us."

Elisabeth knew this herself, and she prayed its reality for her daughter's heart. Still, it was a challenge to keep going forward, not knowing the future—a young single mother and her little girl.

"Did Jesus love my daddy?" Valerie asked. Elisabeth nodded.

"Then why did He let him get killed?"

"I don't know all of the reasons, Val, but I know he was a very good father to you, and that God gave him to you as a blessing, even if only for a very short time."

"Well, I would like to have another daddy, Mommy," Valerie declared. "I'm going to pray He gives me another one, someday. I really hope He will!" Elisabeth was still tall, of course, she was growing older, and she felt somewhat doubtful of the prospects of getting another husband. But she didn't say those things to Valerie.

By this time in her life, Elisabeth knew that sometimes the fear of something doesn't go away and a person must choose to move forward even when he—or she—is afraid.

"Lord, sometimes, I want to lie down and never get up," Elisabeth confessed later that night in her own room. "Give me your grace not to sink into despondency, or a world of cares. Help me to get up and do the next thing." She felt confident, in spite of her fear, that what the Lord had called her to do, He would also enable her to do.

That night, doing the next thing had meant reading a book with her daughter, and intimately discussing their mutual sense of loss. Then the next thing had been to pray together with Valerie and tuck her into bed. In the morning, doing the next thing would mean getting up, scrambling some eggs, and getting Valerie down to the bus stop in time for school. Then it would mean washing the dishes. She imagined that before noon, it would also mean answering some invitations for speaking engagements, making plane reservations, and trapping her thoughts by typewriter onto her next book manuscript. Doing the next thing would keep her up and moving, just like the poem reminded her:

> Many a questioning, many a fear,
> many a doubt hath its quieting here.
> Moment by moment, let down from heaven,
> time, opportunity, guidance are given.
> Fear not tomorrow, child of the King,
> trust that with Jesus, do the next thing.

So that's what she did.

Love has a Price Tag

Not long after, the Lord had a surprise for Valerie. But no one could have been more surprised than Elisabeth herself. Dr Addison Leitch, a professor at a college where Elisabeth had spoken a few times, asked her to marry him. He had lost his wife a few years earlier, and he had daughters that were close to Valerie's age. He loved the Lord; he was intelligent. He taught New Testament and wrote commentaries on its teachings, and he loved books and words, just like Elisabeth. They married in 1969.

"I'm a pointer and an explainer," he said. "It's my job to say, 'do you see this? Do you know what it means'?"[1]

Together, he and Elisabeth wrote books and articles, and they sometimes shared joint speaking engagements. He was a gentleman, and to Elisabeth's delight, they became fast friends. Not knowing whether to be more stunned or grateful, she just settled in to enjoy it. She

---

1. Elisabeth Elliot, *Love Has a Price Tag* (Ann Arbor: Servant Books, 1979), p. 9.

would be a married woman again, after thirteen years
of being a widow!

Valerie was ecstatic. This was a clear answer to her
years-long prayer. She was now thirteen, but right away
she asked if it would be alright with him if she called
him "Daddy."

By now, Elisabeth was a much sought-after speaker
on the subject of missions, Christian commitment,
and the Christian home. But as she spoke around the
country, meeting women in all walks of life—from
Mennonite women in simple head coverings to
scholarly women in academic robes and hats—she
noticed something that concerned her. The feminist
movement was gaining strength. The feminist
movement formed a group of very verbal and powerful
women dissatisfied with marriage and a woman's
place in society. They wanted to change people's ideas
to allow for women to choose careers and leave the
home. Women were told to seek their own happiness
and fulfillment by getting their own careers. Feminists
discouraged women from marrying or having many
children. Men were made to look like tyrants, and
divorce was made to look good. Working only in the
home, feminists told women, was for drab women or
for women who weren't too bright or who were too
fearful to throw off the shackles that bound them there.
It was drudge work. But getting into the corporate
world, having a high paying job—now that was true
talent and true fulfillment.

And then, some very intelligent women claiming to be Christians started speaking out. These women also wanted to embrace feminist ideas. These "Christian feminists" were going after Christian women by trying to twist the Bible's words to make those words say something other than what they meant. Christian women were told that they really don't need to follow their husband's leadership, like the Bible taught—that they can be leaders and providers too.

Elisabeth had experience making her own way in the world. And she had experience as a wife and mother. She felt that feminism tempted women to be ungrateful for the men that God had given them.

Elisabeth also knew that this thinking was wrong-headed at the core. Following the Lord meant giving up our rights to ourselves; it meant following the way of the cross—self-sacrifice and self-denial. She knew that these feminists were glorifying life outside the home, by assuming that a high-paying job would be fun and glamorous and the most fulfilling work a woman could do. But Elisabeth knew that following the Lord meant that women didn't have to push to be like men; they could find the most fulfillment in being women, as God designed them to be. She declared that you could not be a Christian and a feminist at the same time.

She began to receive letters from young women like this.

Dear Mrs Leitch,

I am thirty years old, and I have three small children. Some days are hard. I feel like I have no adult conversation, and that my life consists of cleaning up the floor, the table, and little feet all day long.

I've been told that my brain is going to waste, and that I should get a job. In college, I received an accounting degree. Do you think I should put it to good use?

Elisabeth would respond with something like this.

Dear Mary,

I understand the cultural pull on your life. Yet I challenge the assumption that your brain is wasting away or that you will find fulfillment anywhere outside the will of God.

He designed you for a purpose. You are a woman. Only a woman can bear children. In nurturing the children God has given you to bear and love, you will be fulfilling His purpose for your life. Your mind will find daily opportunities for creativity and strength of thought. And all that you do in the home is an offering to Him. When you wash the dishes, offer it up to the Lord as a service to Him. When you put a little one down to bed, offer your song in worship to the Lord who made all things. There is no higher privilege than serving Him. There is no greater cause to which you can devote your time and talent.

In accepting His will, you will find true peace,
Your friend,
Elisabeth

But Elisabeth had heavier things on her heart. Very shortly after her marriage to Addison Leitch came bad news. Together that winter, the couple sat facing a doctor in a clean, white office furnished with cold metal chairs.

"I am sorry to inform you, Dr Leitch, that you have cancer," the doctor began. "We think that surgery will take care of it, but we can't be sure."

Add and Elisabeth nodded. It was all right. They would trust the Lord.

Over the following months, though, it became evident that surgery was only a temporary fix. The cancer returned, this time more severe.

"We will prescribe more surgery and some radiation," the doctor told them. "We think it's curable."

Back home, Add and Elisabeth talked things over.

"Would you be willing for me to research some healthy eating that might fight your cancer?" asked Elisabeth. She wanted to help this husband of such short acquaintance any way she could.

"Well, what did you have in mind?" Add asked.

"I've been reading about an anti-cancer diet in some nutrition books," she said. "I'd like to prepare you a diet high in leafy green vegetables and broccoli, cabbage and cauliflower—with high doses of Vitamin C."

"That's fine with me," Add acquiesced. "Just make it as tasty as you can."

Elisabeth flew into the work with a missionary zeal. This was a way she could serve God—by serving the husband that God had given her. She was still so grateful for him that she could not think of a possible future without him.

He was still able to carry out his lecturing and writing duties for a while. Sometimes people would ask him, "Dr Leitch, what do you like to do in your free time?"

"Curl up with a good author!"[2] he would reply, laughing. "I live with one I just love."

Elisabeth would smile. She loved his droll sense of humor.

Then came the day when they met with a doctor who had less hopeful words for them.

"We've completed the treatments," he began, "yet the tests show that his cancer continues to return. I am sorry; I'm afraid there is nothing more we can do."

Friends told Elisabeth that they were praying for Addison's healing. They prayed for his peace and comfort.

She felt that neither prayer was answered. Add was enduring a tremendous trial of suffering. But graciously, the Lord had poured out peace on her. It kept her patiently busy tending to Add's needs, cooking him nourishing soups and salads every day, propping up his pillows to make him as comfortable in bed as possible, and bathing his head with a clean white washcloth, now that he was so confined.

"Lord, please give Add some of the peace you've given me," she prayed. Every day, she read Scripture to this godly man, and every day she watched him weaken. Every day, she saw death pursue him like an enemy.

Finally, on his last day, she read Psalm 23 to him. She quoted the last verse of "Guide Me, O Thou Great Jehovah." She took his hand.

2. Ibid.

"Add, dear, is everything all right?"

"Great!" he whispered. She placed a hot water bottle at his feet. "That feels marvelous," he said.

Then Elisabeth heard the words "Jesus Christ" on his lips, very faintly, as if from far away. "He will raise me up," he whispered. Shortly after, he was gone.[3]

The Lord had given his servant peace. And Elisabeth, after just four years of marriage, had lost a dearly-loved husband, once again. She had loved again, and she had lost again. The Lord gave, and the Lord took away. Once again, she bore her grief to the altar of worship.

---

3. Elisabeth Elliot to Folks, September 25, 1973, Folder 9, Box 5, Collection 278, Papers of Elisabeth Howard Elliot, Archives of the Billy Graham Center, Wheaton, Illinois.

A Silver Lining around Dark Clouds

Before Add died, Elisabeth was invited to speak on the college campus where he taught. On one of these occasions, she was invited to address the remarks of a liberal theologian. The students at the school were sure that the professor's wife would be outclassed in an exchange of wits with an accomplished theologian. But she did well. Afterward, as everyone was filing out of the lecture hall, a young man with big hair, wearing jeans and a jacket decked with long fringes, approached her.

"Ma'am, I've never seen anything like what you just did," he said. "You cleaned his clock! I just wish I could hug you."[1]

Elisabeth shook his hand, liking him at once. "Thank you for your encouragement," she said. "My only desire is to stick by what God's Word says."

"I know," he said, hurrying off before he had administered the hug—shy, perhaps, of taking liberties with a well-known personality.

---

1. Quotes by Walt Shepard from the *Elisabeth Elliot Memorial Service Wheaton College*.
https://www.youtube.com/watch?v=WSi3mR9GQIE

As the months passed and Add's home care had become more taxing, Elisabeth decided to post notices around the college, advertising for a young man to board with the Leitches—someone who could help her with the heavy lifting now that Add had grown so helpless.

This same young man appeared on her doorstep one day, but Elisabeth didn't recognize him at first. "I'd like to apply for the job," he said. "I've been a hospital orderly before, and I think I could help."

"I'm a meticulous person," Elisabeth told him in the interview. "Does that pose any problems for you?"[2]

"Um, no ma'am, it doesn't pose any problems at all!"[3] The young man gulped. Maybe he could learn to be a bit tidier, but surely he wasn't too bad.

"Well, Walt, you're hired," she said. "How soon can you move in?"

Add died the day the young man was to move in. Elisabeth immediately posted an advertisement for a second boarder, for propriety's sake. Having a single man in the house with her husband gone would pose problems. A second student answered a couple of days later.

After a couple of weeks there, Elisabeth looked at Walt closely.

"I know you from somewhere,"[4] she exclaimed.

---

2. Ibid.
3. Ibid.
4. Ibid.

"Oh, no, no ma'am, you don't,"[5] Walt tried to throw her off course.

"Yes, I know you from somewhere,"[6] Elisabeth tried to think back.

"I don't think so, ma'am," Walt assured her with a knowing chuckle.

"Yes, now I remember," Elisabeth said. "I just want to know, why didn't you hug me?"[7] They both laughed.

As her driver as well as her boarder, Walt often escorted Elisabeth to speaking engagements. By default, he also acted as her bodyguard in places where she was not so welcome. Sometimes her views about the Bible's authority and what it says to men and women were not too popular. And sometimes Walt's protective nature and his colorful way of speaking proved a little too enthusiastic.

"Walt, I appreciate you sticking up for me, but could you do it with a little less color?"[8] Elisabeth asked him one day when she ducked into the car.

"Yes ma'am!"

In spite of Walt's untidy habits, Elisabeth loved him as if he were her son. He reminded her so much of Jim, she told her family. He had "——the same lust for life, the same earnestness toward God, the same iron-jawed determination not to be turned aside from his

5. Ibid.
6. Ibid.
7. Ibid.
8. Ibid.

calling."[9] He was twenty-eight, the same age Jim was when she'd lost him.

Just after she—and Valerie—met Walt, Elisabeth was impressed with a sense of a common destiny for the two young people. Valerie was eighteen now, and it seemed to Elisabeth, that Walt was developing a consuming fascination with photographs of Valerie. And Valerie, now ready to graduate from high school and head to college, well, she loved him at first sight, from what her mother could tell.

By now, the school where Add once taught had asked Elisabeth to come on as a professor. They appreciated her intellect and Biblical wisdom, and she was an articulate speaker. So she began teaching a class on Christian Expression. The class delved into what Christian expression should look like in speech, writing, and behavior.

She remembered Add's advice. He used to tell his students that "the importance of a thing was in direct ratio to the difficulty in defining it."[10] So Elisabeth decided to give her students an assignment that would help them in delving into the mysteries of God. He created both man and woman in his image, so what did Christianity look like when expressing ourselves specifically as male and female?

9. Elisabeth Elliot to Folks, December 31, 1974, Folder 10, Box 5, Collection 278, Papers of Elisabeth Howard Elliot, Archives of the Billy Graham Center, Wheaton, Illinois.
10. Elisabeth Elliot, *Love Has a Price Tag* (Ann Arbor: Servant Books, 1979), p. 31.

"The assignment for this week is to write a paper defining masculinity and femininity," she told her class one day. "You have a limit of two pages," she went on. "But if you can manage it in two sentences, that will be fine." She doubted they could do it.

When they came back to class two days later, the response was unanimous.

"Mrs Leitch, that was the hardest assignment you've ever given us!" said some.

"In fact," said others, "that may have been the hardest assignment we've ever had."

It was true. How did one go about defining words like "masculine" and "feminine"? Elisabeth continued to travel around the country, speaking and writing on the subject.

The feminists talked about what women want and what women feel, what they've been kept from doing and what they want to do as a result of demanding their "rights." But Elisabeth noticed that these women evaded completely the idea of what women are. And they twisted the Bible's words into minimizing all differences between men and women, other than physical differences. They forced their listeners to make a choice between their interpretation of the Bible and the plain words the apostle Paul had written. They didn't seem very happy with the idea that God had fashioned them as women. But Elisabeth's whole life had been about saying yes to what God fashions.

Let me be a Woman

Elisabeth fed another sheet of paper into her typewriter. This time her manuscript would discuss not only the acceptance, but the delight, of being a woman. And she would tackle the definition—or the essence—of femininity.

"Let Me be a Woman," she titled it, "Notes to my daughter on the meaning of womanhood."

She began by acknowledging that Valerie knew that these notes not only came out of her experience of marriage, "*[t]hey come out of a lifetime, most of which has been spent single (I have been married, you know, for only a seventh of my life). They come out of being a woman, and seeking to be—single, married, widowed—a woman for God.*"[1]

She paused, thinking back. A couple of years had passed since they met Walt. Valerie had been away at college, and their romance had blossomed over the miles. At Christmas-time that year, Walt had come to Elisabeth with a big request.

1. Elisabeth Elliot, *Let Me Be a Woman*, (Wheaton: Tyndale House, 1976), p. 10.

"Ma'am, I'd like to speak with you," he began, sweating just a little. "I-I'd like to ask for your daughter's hand in marriage."

"There is no one to whom I would so gladly give it."[2] She smiled. "But she is close to graduating, Walt. I'd like for her to finish college."

"I know," he said. "I am willing to wait for that."

"It'll be almost a year. Do you think you can stick it out?" she asked.

"Ma'am, I'm a Calvinist,"[3] he said. "I am sure that I can, God helping me."

Elisabeth rejoiced. God had given her daughter a man who believed that God was in control and who trusted Him for the timing. What a treasure!

Now she turned back to Valerie's book, with her thoughts on being God's woman.

"The attitude with which this effort began is summed up in the prayer of Betty Scott Stam, copied into my Bible and signed when I was ten or eleven years old," she typed. Betty's story had stayed with her from her childhood.

"'Lord, I give up all my own plans and purposes, all my own desires and hopes, and accept Thy will for my life. I give myself, my life, my all, utterly to Thee to be Thine forever. Fill me and seal me with Thy Holy Spirit. Use me as Thou wilt, send me where Thou wilt, work out Thy whole will in my life at any cost, now and forever.'"[4]

---

2. Ibid., p. 11.
3. Ibid.
4. Ibid., p. 10.

Over the next several months, she worked long distance with Val on plans for bridesmaid dresses, food for the wedding reception, and the avalanche of wedding gifts that were beginning to pour in. In fits and spurts, she typed as fast as she could on the growing manuscript.

And she finished it just in time to give an early publisher's copy to her daughter to read on her honeymoon. It was leather bound and imprinted with the words, *"To Valerie on the eve of her wedding, May 1, 1976."*

Valerie surprised her mom with a telegram sent from the place where she and Walt were swimming and snorkeling at the Virgin Islands on their honeymoon.

"Your book makes strong Walt weep," she chose the few words she needed. "Love, Val and Walt."[5]

Elisabeth thought back to the conclusion of her book:

"You can't talk about the idea of equality and the idea of self-giving in the same breath. You can talk about partnership, but it is the partnership of the dance. If two people agree to dance together they agree to give and take, one to lead and one to follow. This is what a dance is. Insistence that both lead means there won't be any dance. It is the woman's delighted yielding that gives him freedom ...

"If you can understand your womanhood, Valerie, in this light, you will know fullness of life. Hear the call of God to be a woman. Obey that call. Turn your energies to service.

5. Elisabeth Elliot to Folks, May 7, 1976, Folder 12, Box 5 Collection 278, Papers of Elisabeth Howard Elliot, Archives of the Billy Graham Center, Wheaton, Illinois.

"*Whether your service is to be to a husband and through him, and the family and home God gives you, to serve the world, or whether you should remain, in the providence of God, single in order to service the world without the solace of husband, home and family, you will know fullness of life, fullness of liberty and (I know whereof I speak) fullness of joy.*"[6]

Elisabeth smiled to think of her new son and her daughter, who'd just written to describe herself as the happiest twenty-one-year-old woman in the world. Truly, it was a privilege to be a woman.

6. Elisabeth Elliot, *Let Me Be a Woman*, (Wheaton: Tyndale House, 1976), p. 185.

Yes, I've Heard of Elisabeth Elliot

Elisabeth passed by the living room and saw Lars curiously eyeing her. The coffee table edition of *The Savage my Kinsman* was turned over to the back, where her picture was imprinted just beside a short biographical description. She was pretty sure that Lars had just figured out that his landlady, Mrs Leitch, was also Elisabeth Elliot.

But she went on into the kitchen, pretending not to notice.

Lars Gren was a good boarder. He was the second student who had moved in after Add had died, a couple of days after Walt. He had helped out with Valerie's wedding. In fact, he and the women's Bible study class had basically run the whole reception—and very well, in fact. He was capable with all sorts of fix-it projects too, really handy to have around the house.

Lars also drove Elisabeth places, just like Walt had done. And he was pleasant company to have around.

But at some point—she had not been able to determine just when—the look in Lars' eye hinted at more affection than what you might typically hold for your landlady.

Sure enough, Lars eventually worked up the courage to let her know how much he had come to care for her. It seemed the Lord might give her another husband? Elisabeth was amazed.

But in the future, they never could agree on just how he had approached her in courtship. He always declared that he had stumbled around and extended anything but an eloquent appeal. She always figured out ways during her conference appearances to sing his praises, claiming his advances were manly and winsome. From her lips, his clumsy words came across as downright poetic.

"During this time in my life, when I was single, widowed again, I admitted two boarders to my home," she would say. "And in the providence of God, one of them married my daughter, and the other one married me."

Crowds laughed. Then she continued. "It's hard to say no to a man who tells you as he is courting you that he wants to build fences around you and take care of you and stand on all sides to protect you."

Lars would laugh too. "No, that's not how it went. I was never so articulate."

Then she would tell of her own personal story and how God had led her through losing a husband who was martyred, years of serving on the mission field as a widow, then marriage again with a husband who died of cancer four years after they were married, and finally, her recent marriage to Lars in 1977, a year after Val and Walt were wed.

"Lars is feeling just fine this morning, thank you," she would say. Her humor was understated. "And he is hoping to outlast the first two."

She felt she should put her audience at ease. As a notable person, she was the object of much speculation. And people would get it wrong sometimes.

"Did you know that she's been married three or four times?" some would say in alarm.

"I heard she was married to Hudson Taylor," declared one woman, with authority. Small wonder that Elisabeth found it necessary to sort things out for her listeners. Hudson Taylor was a missionary to China in the 1800s! She wanted to make sure they understood that she was a one-man woman and was solidly committed to marriage, marriage to a husband from this century!

She and Lars had a great many adventures together as she traveled around the world, speaking on purity and waiting on God, on missions and finding God's will, on masculinity and femininity, giving her story.

Wherever they traveled, Lars set up a book table in the back of the auditorium. There at the back, his winsome Southern charm forged abundant friendships for the two of them. And he sold a lot of books, helping her ministry to reach more young people as she grew older.

One evening, a young man approached Lars, wanting to ask Elisabeth some questions. Lars took him over to where she was standing.

"I have been wondering about marriage," he began. "I want to be married."

"Well, do you have someone in mind?" Elisabeth asked.

"Yes," he answered.

"Tell me about her."

Then he went into great detail, describing her godly attributes to Elisabeth.

"I think she sounds lovely and would make a wonderful wife," Elisabeth encouraged. "What's stopping you?"

"I suppose the time and the place," the young man replied

"Well, what about here? And now?" Elisabeth was direct. After all these years, her answers were still straightforward, no fluff allowed.

But even she was surprised to see what happened next. The boy walked immediately over to a group of girls. One of the girls caught his coming with a sparkle in her eye. He knelt down on one knee in front of that one.

"Will you marry me?" he asked, in front of a whole crowd of people. Elisabeth, watching, almost jumped out of her skin.

"Yes, I will," the girl answered, not at all flustered. The surrounding young people clapped their hands and cheered.

Back in their hotel room, Elisabeth was mortified. "What have I done, Lars?" she asked. "I had no idea that would happen."

Lars chuckled, but nodded his surprise too.

"What if it's a disaster?" she exclaimed. "What if the marriage is unhappy—will I be responsible?"

As the Lord would have it though, the couple did get married. They served the Lord overseas and in the States. They had children and the young man became a respected youth pastor. They even became the Grens' neighbors for a time, years later, and kept in touch.

Elisabeth could breathe a sigh of relief.

Still Learning

Elisabeth closed the sagging scrapbook and sat down on her sofa. The gaggle of girls gathered around her on the floor rose to leave.

"It's been a wonderful afternoon here with you and Mr Gren," one of them said. "Thank you so much for opening your home to us."

"Did you sign your name in our guest book?" Lars asked. "Don't get out the door without that."

"We did," chimed in all of the girls. "We passed it around the room earlier."

Guests had filled up book after book of thanks for the Grens' hospitality over the years. People from all around the world had come to listen to Elisabeth relate again and again the story of the Lord's dealings with the Waorani. She would retrieve heavy albums from under the antique buffet and leaf through the rough, black pages, where black and white photos showed wide-faced Indians with straight-cropped black hair and round wooden plugs in their ears—and always a sprightly blond toddler, romping among them. The people in the photos lay in airy hammocks or crouched before crude fires, backed by walls of tree-limbs trying desperately to attain a vertical. Manicured American guests would watch this woman, scrapbooks in hand, who had endured so much, speak of God's rule and His love in the same breath, accepting both uncritically. Her story still spoke.

Behind her, lining the whole of one side of their house, almost floor to ceiling windows framed her swept-back bun as she spoke. You could see small schooners out beyond her, down the rocky coast where they lived, north of Boston. There were old crochet throws across the sofa, comfortable in the same room displaying exotic South American artifacts—a fan dangling from the hearth, made of the purple plumes of an Ecuadorian bird, on the mantle, small primitive tools, fashioned of wood or stone. There was a long thin spear that lay casually along the hallway atop an old radiator, still declaring itself foreign and out of context to its New England surroundings.

Lars closed the door as the last of the girls left. As Elisabeth gathered up the tea cups, Lars picked up the spear to put it by the hearth. He dropped it, clattering it against the edge of the woodstove.

Elisabeth was tired after hosting company, and ready to go to bed. "Be careful, Lars!" she snapped at her husband. She'd been married for years now to Lars, and they were pretty comfortable with each other. "Don't you know how old that thing is?"

"Well, you don't need to get bent out of shape about it," he retorted.

But this time, Elisabeth was sure that Lars was the one who was wrong—he needed to apologize.

That night, she closeted herself in the little study off their bedroom and opened her Bible. She turned to 1 Corinthians 13, the love chapter. She tried her name beside each of the descriptions. Patient? Kind? Not easily provoked?

No, when she put her name in the place of the word "love" in the passage, it came out more like this: "Elisabeth loses patience, is destructive, possessive, anxious to impress, cherishes inflated ideas of her own importance, has bad manners, pursues selfish advantage, is touchy, keeps account of evil. ..."[1]

She immediately saw things in a new light. After all, hadn't she prayed that the Lord would make her the kind of wife that she ought to be? Here the Lord had given her a third husband—a third opportunity to learn afresh and deeply what it meant to love, to lay her life down in submission to His ways. Should she not receive it?

She realized that her annoyance with Lars was a petty thing. She didn't need Lars to apologize; she needed to learn more about love. This kind of love *"knows no limit to its endurance, no end to its trust, no fading of its hope; it can outlast anything. It is, in fact, the one thing that still stands when all else has fallen (1 Corinthians 13:7-8 PHILLIPS)."*

---

1. Elisabeth Elliot, *Love Has a Price Tag* (Ann Arbor: Servant Books, 1979), p. 111.

This attitude opened up all kinds of opportunities for Elisabeth. She was still a learner, and every day she had new things to talk about that the Lord was showing her, teaching her, convicting her of—new things that could encourage women in all walks of life.

In 1988, she was asked to host a radio program called *Gateway to Joy*. There, her resonant voice began daily to go out over the airwaves, describing to her listeners the stories of her life, old and new, which would encourage others in their walk with the Lord. Themes of suffering and worship and giving your all to the Lord undergirded all her stories. She won her listeners to the thought that every suffering and every distress, when yielded to the Lord, becomes not only a way to worship but a gateway to the Lord Himself— with all the joy that comes along with that.

"I have loved you with an everlasting love (NIV)." Elisabeth opened every program with this passage from Jeremiah 31. And every program closed with, "This is your friend, Elisabeth Elliot." Reruns of the program can still be heard online for listeners of this generation.

This season of her life was fruitful and full. She sent out a bi-monthly publication of her thoughts—called the *Elisabeth Elliot Newsletter*. She wrote more books, eventually totaling over twenty. There were the books she wrote on the time she spent in Ecuador and her book explaining femininity. Then she added a book on masculinity that she wrote for her nephew, and books on loneliness, suffering, discipline, finding the right spouse, and finding God's will. She helped produce a video series on what a Christian home looks like, with the help of her daughter Valerie and her eight lively grandchildren. She wrote biographies of her dear Jim and of her old heroine Amy Carmichael. She contributed articles and scholarly treatises for Christian magazines. She helped make a documentary about the Waorani and her missionary friends from long ago. She corresponded with hundreds of people. She granted dozens of interviews. She hosted her grandchildren to the Cove and treated them to her homemade chicken soups and trips to the hardware store. All kinds of household projects were fun to do with "Granny." And all projects were laced with lessons of organization and efficiency.

She still took speaking engagements, not only to almost every state in the United States, but also to far-flung countries: England, Holland, Germany, Hungary, and several trips back down to Ecuador.

The Final Surrender

As Elisabeth grew older, it became more difficult for her to construct a well-honed sentence. Sometimes she couldn't find the words she was searching for, and she began forgetting people's names and coming up blank on topics she wanted to discuss.

A visit to the doctor brought her news that was hard to hear. She was experiencing dementia, an illness of old age that attacks the mind. In 2001, at age seventy-four, she had to give up speaking on the radio—the time seemed so short that she had been on the air—and she had thrived in this ministry. Then in 2004, she stopped accepting speaking engagements altogether.

She and Lars still traveled and visited friends for a while. But the forthright Elisabeth began to fade. Eventually, she and Lars stayed home most of the time. Their home was a place of solace to them.

Upstairs, in her small study off their bedroom, a typewriter lay dusty on a massive cherry wood desk. Her pen, the phone, her calendar were silent now. The massive windows still gazed quietly down on the ocean cove, before which she had once gained daily inspiration for her writing. Childhood photos of Valerie smiled through the emptiness. Classic volumes of literature, from Plutarch to Flannery O'Conner, once loved and well used, now lay stiffly on the shelves.

Most days now, Lars would prop her up in her favorite rocking chair and sit and talk to her, helping her recall all the memories they shared together. One of his favorite memories happened on a day he came up from his office to talk with Elisabeth about something.

"I have a thought," he had begun.

"Well, hang on to it—it's in a strange place!" she had teased. He still chuckled over her quick wit as he reminisced. Together they had enjoyed many inside jokes over the years.

She would never speak of her life-long ministry in terms of success or failure—only the Lord could judge that. She had seen her failures and disappointments all through. But they laughed together and joked, and marveled at the Lord's faithfulness to them. Other times, now, Lars would carefully position her in a wheelchair, place a broad-brimmed, floppy hat on her head, and strike out down the hilly neighborhood streets or the Magnolia bushes behind their house. He was her constant companion.

Some said that dementia had robbed her of her greatest gift—her mind. But Elisabeth knew that wasn't true. All she wanted, all she had ever wanted, was the Lord's will. On that premise, following Him was all she had ever wanted to do, and getting Him was her greatest gift. She would see Him soon, she knew.

The Christian world hadn't forgotten her. One day, WORLD Magazine sent a reporter to chat with Lars and Elisabeth about their rich history of work in the kingdom of Jesus Christ, and how she faced her most recent challenge—this dementia of her old age.

The reporter watched as Elisabeth strained to communicate with her husband, mostly by facial expression and barely perceptible hand movements. At this point in the progression of the disease, Elisabeth was non-verbal. Lars recounted her story for her, as he and the reporter chatted through the morning. He talked about her time on the mission field. He told stories about their travels. He described their courtship and marriage, now over thirty years past. Then he quoted the verse from Isaiah 43:2 that had revived her weary spirit during her illness.

"When you pass through the waters, I will be with you; and through the rivers, they will not overwhelm you. When you walk through the fire, you will not be scorched, nor will the flame burn you (AMP).*"*

It was the same passage that had comforted her years and years before as a young woman in her twenties, when she had lost Jim.

They talked on. Elisabeth's mind drifted in and out.

She roused in time to hear the interviewer ask Lars, "And how has Elisabeth handled this most recent ordeal—dementia?" Their voices seemed far away.

"She has handled the illness just as she did the deaths of her husbands," she heard Lars say.

"She accepted those things, [knowing] they were no surprise to God," he said. "It was something she would rather not have experienced, but she received it."[1]

For the first time that morning, Elisabeth focused her clear blue eyes on the woman, and she nodded as hard as she could. "Yes."[2] It was the only word she could force from her lips during the entire interview, so she rallied all of her fading energies into getting it out.

It said enough.

---

1. Used by permission, WORLD magazine, *Walking Through Fire* by Tiffany Owens, March 8, 2014, www.wng.org
2. Ibid.

Beyond the Gates of Splendor

When the end came, her husband Lars was by Elisabeth's side, singing one of her favorite hymns by Anna Waring.

> In heav'nly love abiding,
> No change my heart shall fear;
> And safe is such confiding,
> For nothing changes here.
> The storm may roar about me,
> My heart may low be laid,
> But God is round about me,
> And can I be dismayed?

How strange that Lars found the hymn a few days later typed up on an index card, autographed by her graceful hand twenty years earlier:

> *For my dearest, April 24, 1995.*
> *This is what we count on!*
> *With love, Elisabeth."*

Lars had discovered it in one of his old Bibles that he had not used in a while. It seemed a message from her, lingering after her departure.

"*At 6:15 on the morning of June 15, 2015, Elisabeth Elliot died,*" wrote her friend John Piper.

"It is a blunt sentence for a blunt woman. This is near the top of why I felt such an affection and admiration for her. Blunt — not ungracious, not impetuous, not snappy or gruff. But direct, unsentimental, no-nonsense, tell-it-like-it-is, no whining allowed. Just pull your britches on and go die for Jesus."

---

1. John Piper, *"Peaches in Paradise:Why I Loved Elisabeth Elliot,* Desiring God Ministries, http://www.desiringgod.org/articles/peaches-in-paradise

Tributes

Notes and tributes from people all over the world poured in, by mail, by blog, by Facebook post. Men and women remembered her courage on the mission field, her open-hearted forgiveness of her husband's murderers, her constant willingness to love and serve in the midst of sorrow, her solid determination to stick to the Bible when others waffled, and her intelligent blending of theology and life in a way that won you to the Lord's way. Christian leaders spoke out, describing all the ways she had influenced them in their ministries. Wives and mothers described the difference her teaching had made in their homes.

She was buried in a simple coffin in a cemetery full of neatly carved blocks of gravestones, many from the civil war. Her gravestone was different—a smooth, rounded but uncut rock. On one side was inscribed:

Addison Hardie Leitch—
loved husband and best friend of Elisabeth

followed by a quote from poet John Milton,

For we to Him indeed all praises owe and daily thanks. I
chiefly who enjoyed so far the happier lot, enjoying thee,
preeminent by so much odds.

But on Elisabeth's side of the stone, the inscription is direct and simple:

> *Elisabeth Elliot Gren,*
> *December 21, 1926–June 15, 2015*
> *When thou passest through the waters,*
> *I will be with thee (Isaiah 43:2).*

These words had comforted her a half a century before, when she was a young woman looking into what she thought might be a lonely future, but for the Lord helping her. He had helped her, more than she could ever ask or think. And He had walked faithfully with her in so many, many ways for her whole life long.

It was all she had ever longed for—to be welcomed into the Lord's presence and to be close to Him. And after eighty-eight years, it was what she gained, forever.

Elisabeth Elliot
Timeline

1926:   Elisabeth Howard born December 21 in Brussels, Belgium.

1927:   The Howards return to the States to Philadelphia, Pennsylvania.

1933:   John and Betty Stam visit the Howard home.

1940:   Elisabeth attends Hampden-Dubose Academy and discovers Amy Carmichael.

1944:   Elisabeth goes to Wheaton College to study classical Greek and linguistics in the hope of the going to the mission field.

1947:   Elisabeth meets Jim Elliot.

1948:   Elisabeth graduates from Wheaton College.

1951:   Elisabeth works as a single missionary among the Quichua and Colorado Indians.

1953:   Jim Elliot and Elisabeth are married in Ecuador. They work together in Puyupungu and Shandia.

1955:   The missionaries initiate contact with the savage Auca tribe, and daughter Valerie is born to Jim and Elisabeth.

1956:   Jim Elliot and four fellow missionaries are martyred by Auca spears. Elisabeth writes *Through Gates of Splendor*. It becomes a bestseller. Hundreds of young people, inspired by the story, give their lives to go to the mission field.

1958:   Elisabeth and Rachel Saint live among the Auca tribes, now known as Waorani, translating Scripture and evangelizing.

1961:   Elisabeth writes *The Savage My Kinsman* recording her life among the Waorani.

1963:   Elisabeth returns to the States and lives with Valerie in Franconia, New Hampshire.

1966:   Elisabeth writes her only novel, giving her philosophy of missions: *No Graven Image*.

1969: Elisabeth marries Addison Leitch.

1973: Addison Leitch dies.

1974: Elisabeth is appointed to adjunct professor for Gordon-Conwell Theological Seminary and teaches a course called "Christian Expression" for several years.

1975: Elisabeth attends Evangelical Women's Caucus and learns about "Christian" feminism. She begins speaking out in favor of God's biblical design for women. She also writes *These Strange Ashes,* recording her time with the Colorado Indians.

1976: Daughter Valerie marries Walt Shepard. Elisabeth writes *Let Me Be a Woman* and gives it to Valerie as a wedding gift.

1977: Elisabeth marries Lars Gren. In the decades that follow, he travels with her to many speaking engagements, aiding her in widely distributing her books. Over the years, hundreds of people visit their home in Magnolia, Massachusetts, and the Grens host them to tea and lively discussions of purity, manhood, womanhood, and the re-telling of the story of all the Lord did with the witness of Jim and the Waorani.

1981: Elisabeth writes *The Mark of a Man.*

1984: Elisabeth writes *Passion and Purity*, encouraging young people to give God control of their love lives, and telling the story of her courtship with Jim Elliot.

1988-2001: Elisabeth broadcasts her radio messages on Gateway to Joy.

2005: Elisabeth cuts back her speaking engagements as she slowly succumbs to dementia. Her husband Lars cares for her in their Magnolia, Massachusetts home: 10 Strawberry Cove. Others who'd been blessed by her ministry come alongside Lars to assist in her care.

2015: Elisabeth Elliot dies.

Thinking Further Topics

1.   Missionary From the Start

Do you think it's good for a missionary to feel up to the job? The example that Elisabeth's mother set, by her focus on Philippians 4:13, can teach us that it is a good idea to feel our weakness, because it will keep us depending on the strength of the Lord.

Also, the invention of the airplane was used by the Lord to spread the gospel even further in our world. Can you think of another time in history that an invention was greatly instrumental in spreading God's Word? (Hint: the year 1455).

2.   An Eye for Detail

How did God show Elisabeth His loving and personal care of her? Think about her father, family devotions, and answers to prayer. How does He show his personal care to you, in your life?

Also, the Lord used Elisabeth's father to teach her to listen well to bird calls. How do you think this prepared her for the work she was to do in the future, when she went to the mission field?

3.   Disobedience During Singing

Teaching obedience to their children was top priority for the Howard parents. They believed that a well-disciplined child is a happy child, and that he will grow up to listen to the Lord and serve Him fruitfully, rather than serving his own selfish desires. Look up John 14: 21. What did Betty Scott Stam teach Elisabeth about obedience?

4. Good Missionary Training

Elisabeth felt that missionary life should not be glamorized and that missionaries should not be put up on a pedestal. She knew they were just regular, sinful people, depending on the Lord. This is what she liked about the writing of Amy Carmichael—Amy was so truthful about things. Give an example from the chapter of how Elisabeth thought people should talk about missions and missionaries.

5. A Pure Passion

Elisabeth wanted more than anything for every aspect of her life to reflect her obedience to the Lord, even her "love life." She refused even to "fall in love" without God's firm direction. In our culture, people believe they can't help who they fall in love with. But Elisabeth shows us an example of someone who would only fall in love when it was okay with the Lord. How do you think she accomplished this?

6. A Passion Denied

Read Genesis 22:1-19. This passage teaches us that no person, no matter how dear to us, can take the place of the Lord or stand in the way of our obeying the Lord, even when it's very hard. How did Elisabeth and Jim consistently show they were willing to sacrifice even their most precious relationship in order to serve the Lord?

7. When the Lord Builds the House

This and the next chapter show how Elisabeth learned that God had the right to bless or to withhold blessing from her efforts to translate the gospel for the Colorado Indians. She had expected the Lord would use her; after all, she was sacrificing a lot to be a missionary.

8. When the Lord Destroys What He has Built

The loss of months of Bible translation work was a confusing thing for Elisabeth. But the Lord taught her that He had a right to do what He wanted with her service, whether it looked like success or failure. Her job was to obey; she didn't need to worry about the results of her obedience. Rather than hurting her faith, the events served to strengthen her faith. If we struggle with pride and self-importance, we probably *would* have our faith threatened by such circumstances. What do you think?

9. Yokefellows With a Vision

Chief Atanasio and his people received the gospel given to them by Jim and Elisabeth. This showed Elisabeth that the same effort might succeed with one group that failed with another. God was in control, and only He could save. Look up Puyupungu, Shandia, and other places the Elliots served on the map.

10. New Horizons

A pioneer is one who first enters a region to settle it, thus opening it up for others to come along after. How were Jim, Elisabeth, and their friends pioneers for the gospel? How can you pioneer some gospel work in your own neighborhood?

11. Operation Auca

As Jim and Elisabeth and their friends began plans to reach the Auca tribes for Christ, they discussed the prospect of being killed. After all, the Aucas were killers and had killed. What made them decide to go ahead with "Operation Auca"? What did they decide to bring with them or not bring with them? Make a list of things you think would be important to bring on a gospel expedition like this.

12. Taking Christmas to the Savages

Read Isaiah 43:1,2. Elisabeth relied on this Scripture as she awaited news about the fate of her husband and friends. This Scripture is also inscribed on the rock at her gravesite today. She often relied on the truth of this passage through the many trials in her life. She knew that ultimately, she would not be overcome, no matter how hard things got. See if you can memorize these two verses.

13. Through Gates of Splendor

Do you think that Operation Auca was a success or a failure? Seen through human eyes, it could look like failure. But God used the death of these missionaries to inspire hundreds of people to become missionaries. So what can God do with what appears to be failure in our eyes? Look up 2 Corinthians 12:9,10. On Youtube, watch "Beyond the Gates of Splendor," a documentary telling the story of the Waorani tribe in the years since the killing of the missionaries.

14. Do The Next Thing

All during the time Elisabeth and Jim were serving as missionaries, Elisabeth had a gift that was not being used: her ability to write books. God decides the course our lives take and which gifts He will use. She wasn't pushing herself forward as an author to use her gifts: the opportunity chased her down! Do you accept opportunities God gives you to use your gifts to serve Him?

15. The Savage, My Kinsman

Elisabeth became very famous for being the missionary that went to live with the very tribe that murdered her husband. Do you think you could forgive someone who killed one of your family? She wanted not only to forgive, but also to live among them and help them come to know Jesus. Surely, the Lord gave her much love!

16. Doing the Next Thing Back Home

Have you ever been so sad, that you felt you could not do anything? Or have you ever felt so overwhelmed you didn't know what to do? Discuss how the Lord used the poem "Do the Next Thing" to comfort and help Elisabeth. Do you think that making your bed or washing the dishes can be God's blessed will for us during hard times? Elisabeth teaches us that the answer to this question is "yes"!

17. Love Has a Price Tag

What is the difference between God's design for women and the world's design for women? Feminists tried to make God's design look boring and unfulfilling. They tried to make their own made-up ideas look fun and exciting. Can you think of a biblical example of someone else who did this? (Hint: read Genesis 3). What do you think is wonderful about how God made you, (as a boy or as a girl)?

18. A Silver Lining Around Dark Clouds

The death of her second husband provided yet another opportunity for Elisabeth to learn acceptance of God's will, even when it was not what she wanted. How did Elisabeth apply these same lessons to accepting God's design for women? She believed that we would find our greatest happiness in accepting God's will, even if it is different from our own ideas about what would be fun.

19. Let Me Be a Woman

Elisabeth believed that in submitting to the rule of Scripture, we find true freedom. Rather than being limiting, rules are freeing! Explain how this works. You can use her example of a dance.

20. Yes, I've Heard of Elisabeth Elliot

Elisabeth became a well-known speaker, asked to speak in many churches and countries. Do you think it's tempting to let opportunities like that "go to your head"? How do you think Elisabeth stayed humble before the Lord?

21. Still Learning

After reading this chapter, think of some ways God took Elisabeth's suffering and turned it to good. See Romans 8:28. Write down some of your own challenges and how you see God working good through them.

22. The Final Surrender

The lessons we learn in life will serve us well in death. How was this true for Elisabeth? How do you think Elisabeth would have us remember her? What would you like to be remembered for?

About the Author

Selah Helms is a pastor's wife, mother, and grandmother living in Fort Worth, Texas. After home-schooling her four children, she became an avid history buff, especially interested in medieval, reformation, church history, American Civil War, and World War II studies. When her children were small, she and a friend authored a series of children's books (see Big Bible Answers) designed to help children understand the concepts of the Protestant catechism by illustrating theological truths with stories from church history.

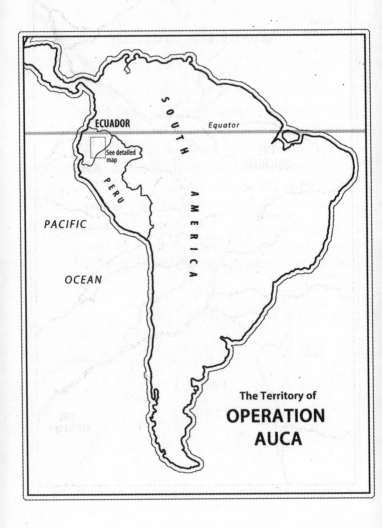

ECUADOR

See detailed map

PERU

PACIFIC

OCEAN

SOUTH AMERICA

Equator

The Territory of
**OPERATION
AUCA**

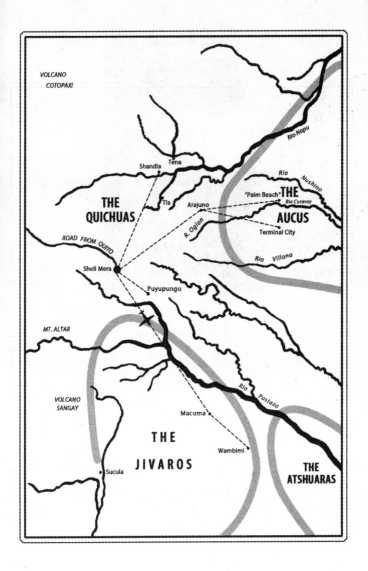

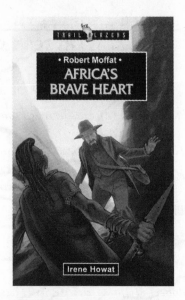

Robert Moffat: Africa's Brave Heart
by Irene Howat

Robert Moffat could think on his feet, and use his hands. He was strong, practical and just the sort of guy you needed to back you up when you were in difficulty. Not only that, he had courage – loads of it, and a longing to bring the good news of Jesus Christ to the people of Africa.

As Robert faced the dangers of drought, wild animals and even the daggers and spears of the people he had come to help, he used his unique collection of gifts and attributes to spread the gospel.

Africa's brave heart blazed a trail into the unknown, starting a work in that continent that continues today.

ISBN: 978-1-84550-715-2

OTHER BOOKS IN THE
TRAIL BLAZERS SERIES

Augustine, The Truth Seeker
ISBN 978-1-78191-296-6
John Calvin, After Darkness Light
ISBN 978-1-78191-550-9
Fanny Crosby, The Blind Girl's Song
ISBN 978-1-78191-163-1
John Knox, The Sharpened Sword
ISBN 978-1-78191-057-3
Eric Liddell, Finish the Race
ISBN 978-1-84550-590-5
Martin Luther, Reformation Fire
ISBN 978-1-78191-521-9
Robert Moffat, Africa's Brave Heart
ISBN 978-1-84550-715-2
D.L. Moody, One Devoted Man
ISBN 978-1-78191-676-6
Mary of Orange, At the Mercy of Kings
ISBN 978-1-84550-818-0
Patrick of Ireland: The Boy who Forgave
ISBN: 978-1-78191-677-3
John Stott, The Humble Leader
ISBN 978-1-84550-787-9
Ulrich Zwingli, Shepherd Warrior
ISBN 978-1-78191-803-6

For a full list of Trail Blazers, please see our
website: www.christianfocus.com
All Trail Blazers are available as e-books

Start collecting this series now!

Ten Boys who used their Talents:
ISBN 978-1-84550-146-4
Paul Brand, Ghillean Prance, C.S.Lewis,
C.T. Studd, Wilfred Grenfell, J.S. Bach,
James Clerk Maxwell, Samuel Morse,
George Washington Carver, John Bunyan.

Ten Girls who used their Talents:
ISBN 978-1-84550-147-1
Helen Roseveare, Maureen McKenna,
Anne Lawson, Harriet Beecher Stowe,
Sarah Edwards, Selina Countess of Huntingdon,
Mildred Cable, Katie Ann MacKinnon,
Patricia St. John, Mary Verghese.

Ten Boys who Changed the World:
ISBN 978-1-85792-579-1
David Livingstone, Billy Graham, Brother Andrew,
John Newton, William Carey, George Müller,
Nicky Cruz, Eric Liddell, Luis Palau,
Adoniram Judson.

Ten Girls who Changed the World:
ISBN 978-1-85792-649-1
Corrie Ten Boom, Mary Slessor,
Joni Eareckson Tada, Isobel Kuhn,
Amy Carmichael, Elizabeth Fry, Evelyn Brand,
Gladys Aylward, Catherine Booth, Jackie Pullinger.

Ten Boys who Made a Difference:
ISBN 978-1-85792-775-7
Augustine of Hippo, Jan Hus, Martin Luther,
Ulrich Zwingli, William Tyndale, Hugh Latimer,
John Calvin, John Knox, Lord Shaftesbury,
Thomas Chalmers.

Ten Girls who Made a Difference:
ISBN 978-1-85792-776-4
Monica of Thagaste, Catherine Luther,
Susanna Wesley, Ann Judson, Maria Taylor,
Susannah Spurgeon, Bethan Lloyd-Jones,
Edith Schaeffer, Sabina Wurmbrand,
Ruth Bell Graham.

Ten Boys who Made History:
ISBN 978-1-85792-836-5
Charles Spurgeon, Jonathan Edwards,
Samuel Rutherford, D L Moody,
Martin Lloyd Jones, A W Tozer, John Owen,
Robert Murray McCheyne, Billy Sunday,
George Whitfield.

Ten Girls who Made History:
ISBN 978-1-85792-837-2
Ida Scudder, Betty Green, Jeanette Li,
Mary Jane Kinnaird, Bessie Adams,
Emma Dryer, Lottie Moon, Florence Nightingale,
Henrietta Mears, Elisabeth Elliot.

Ten Boys who Didn't Give In:
ISBN 978-1-84550-035-1
Polycarp, Alban, Sir John Oldcastle
Thomas Cranmer, George Wishart,
James Chalmers, Dietrich Bonhoeffer,
Nate Saint, Ivan Moiseyev,
Graham Staines.

Ten Girls who Didn't Give In:
ISBN 978-1-84550-036-8
Blandina, Perpetua, Lady Jane Grey,
Anne Askew, Lysken Dirks, Marion Harvey,
Margaret Wilson, Judith Weinberg,
Betty Stam, Esther John.

CHRISTIAN FOCUS PUBLICATIONS

Christian Focus | Christian Heritage | CF4K | Mentor

Christian Focus Publications publishes books for adults and children under its four main imprints: Christian Focus, CF4K, Mentor and Christian Heritage. Our books reflect our conviction that God's Word is reliable and Jesus is the way to know him, and live for ever with him.

Our children's publication list includes a Sunday School curriculum that covers pre-school to early teens, and puzzle and activity books. We also publish personal and family devotional titles, biographies and inspirational stories that children will love.

If you are looking for quality Bible teaching for children then we have an excellent range of Bible stories and age-specific theological books.

From pre-school board books to teenage apologetics, we have it covered!

Find us at our web page:
www.christianfocus.com

CF4·K
Because you're never
too young to know Jesus